At Home with Dying

At Home with Dying

A ZEN

HOSPICE

APPROACH

ଈଚ

Merrill Collett

Shambhala
Boston & London
1999

Shambhala Publications, Inc.
Horticultural Hall
300 Massachusetts Avenue
Boston, Massachusetts 02115
http://www.shambhala.com

Published by arrangement with Andrews McMeel Publishing

9 8 7 6 5 4 3 2 1
Printed in the United States of America
⊗ This edition is printed on acid-free paper that meets the
American National Standards Institute Z39.48 Standard.
Distributed in the United States by Random House, Inc.,
and in Canada by Random House of Canada Ltd

Permissions appear on page 241

Library of Congress Cataloging-in-Publication Data

Collett, Merrill.
[Stay close and do nothing]
At home with dying: a Zen hospice approach/Merrill
Collett.—
1st ed.
p. cm.
Originally published: Stay close and do nothing. Kansas City:
Andrews McMeel Pub., ©1997.
Includes bibliographical references and index.
ISBN 1–57062–515–8 (pbk.: alk. paper)
1. Terminal care.   2. Terminal care—Religious aspects.
3. Terminal care—Psychological
aspects.   4. Death—Religious
aspects—Zen Buddhism.   I. Title.
[R726.8.C64   1999]
362.1'75—dc21   99–24856
CIP

For Mel Weitsman

A monk in the world, the best thing for both.

ళ౨

꿎

Contents

I. Beginner's Mind

One

The Hospice Model of Home Care ✦ Hospice in America ✦ The Ostrich Model of Dying ✦ Choosing Home Care ✦ Choosing to Be a Caregiver ✦ Pain Management ✦ Caregiving as Opportunity ✦ How We Change ✦ Caregiving as Practice

Two

Spiritual Care is Practical Care ✦ How We Die—A Scenario ✦ Dying as Healing ✦ Giving Spiritual Care ✦ Receiving Spiritual Care ✦ Death Doesn't Have to Be "Good"

Three

Two Kinds of Meditation ✦ How to Practice Do-Nothing Meditation ✦ Just Do It ✦ Caregiving and Meditation ✦ Meditation and Death

II. Caregiver's Mind

III. *Inquiring Mind*

When something is
dying it is the greatest teacher.

Shunryu Suzuki-roshi,
speaking not long before his death

ॐ

Acknowledgments

A FAMILIAR BUDDHIST MEAL CHANT BEGINS, "Innumerable labors brought us this food." *At Home with Dying* arrives in exactly that way. There is not a single idea in this book that I can claim as uniquely mine. Nevertheless, it is my hope that what I've written will reach the reader with all the force of a first time. If that should happen to you, please join me in giving thanks to the following people for inspiring my writing:

◆ The Zen teachers Norman Fischer, Paul Haller, Blanche and Lou Hartman, Maylie Scott, and Hekizan Tom Girardot, who died while I was writing this book

◆ The past and present Zen Hospice Project staff members Marcy Bahr, Dan Kuziej, Eileen Lemus, Terry Lesser, Oga Marsch, Anandi Nelson, Frank Ostaseski, Eric Poché, and Harriet Posthuma

◆ The Laguna Honda Hospice staff members Derek Kerr, M.D., Nahidi Mansoureh, R.N., Sahnta Pannutti, and Paul Kelley, M.S.W.

◆ My fellow hospice volunteers Stephanie Amsden, Bobby Atchison, Susan Bistline, Carolyn Botts, Robin Castano, Cathy Crafton, Anne Dorsey, Laureen Elizabeth, Dolly Gattozzi, Marsha Gillespie, Richard Hale, Bill Jaynes, Melissa Kay, Jay Linderman, Anado McLauchlin, Ken McLean, Jerry Miller, Russ Mitchell, Judy Pruzinsky, Isabella Salzman, Pete Sketchley, Cheryl Skinner, Hart Sprager, Louis Vega, Wendy Wank, Alan Waugh, Laura Worden, and Dan Young

✦ Dale Borglum, executive director of the Living/Dying Project in Marin County, California

✦ Fleet Maull, founder of the National Prison Hospice Association

✦ My friends Steve Ajay, Darlene Cohen, Walter Graze, Sue Moon, Bette Silver, Judy Smith, and Roberto Toscano

✦ My partner, the always astonishing Alexandra Frappier

✦ My father, who faithfully cared for a bedridden wife through the years I was doing hospice work and writing this book

✦ My sons, Gabriel and Nathan Collett

A special thanks to Bob Anderson, R.N., Paul Haller, Susan O'Connell, Douglas Penick, and Cathleen Williams for reading and commenting on portions of this book. Thanks also to my literary agent, Charlotte Sheedy, for her strong commitment to this project, and to Christine Schillig, of Andrews McMeel Publishing, for her adept editing.

Above all I want to thank the many people who shared their dying with me. To protect their privacy I've altered the names and circumstances of most of them. In three cases I've used real names: Leroy Hithe, Brian Toole, and David Wells. These were friends with whom I discussed the book and who agreed to be mentioned in it. By including their names, I intend to honor both them and those who remain nameless. But every death is worthy of honor, and every dying person is an eloquent teacher. Now that it's my turn to talk, may I speak for them all.

Introduction

ACCOMPANYING A DYING PERSON to the last breath can be a long and difficult journey, but when we get there we find ourselves changed. We begin wanting to help and we end simply wanting to be. Looking at life from the perspective of death, embracing our transience, we stop straining to make each moment more enjoyable and start savoring existence itself.

At Home with Dying is both a practical manual and a spiritual guide. It combines the most current techniques of hospice care with Eastern wisdom teachings in a step-by-step explanation of how to care for the terminally ill in a way that transforms the caregiver. Among the target readers are the adult children of dying parents; the families and friends of people with AIDS; hospice, bereavement, and religious workers—both volunteer and professional; dying people who want to tell others how they can help; and anyone with an interest in the lessons death teaches.

Home is where the heart is. Most of us would rather die at home, surrounded by the things we know and cared for by the people who love us. But that's not how most terminal care is structured in the United States. The majority of Americans die in the sterile environment of hospitals attended by hurried doctors and nurses.

When we help a friend or loved one die at home we give a great gift. This book seeks to make that gift possible by providing practical instructions for solving the nitty-gritty problems of home caregiving.

There are many of them. Dying is a physical and emotional process of vast complexity, and the caregiver must learn many new things, but everyone is born with the essential skills. These are the capacities to listen, to learn, and to love.

Caregiving takes us back to the basics. Once you start the work, you'll be amazed at how fast it clears away extraneous issues and sets the right priorities. Taking care of a dying person is a great opportunity for getting to know who you really are.

Seeing death as a source of opportunity is not the Western way. Our society rests on the scientific principles of seventeenth-century rationalism, which separated mind from matter. Since the end of matter was considered the end of everything, death was seen as not a part of life but rather its enemy. In making this assumption, science exceeded its authority. Death does not fall within the jurisdiction of science to define. Death is primarily a spiritual, rather than a material, event. To explore death's domain we need as a guide the intuitive eye of the spirit.

Some people cultivate spiritual insight by going to church or synagogue. Others move in less traditional directions, but ultimately all paths lead to surrender. We entrust ourselves to that which sustains us, whether it be God or Jesus or Buddha or Allah or the Goddess or Truth or Love. We invest everything in our deepest belief, and we are rewarded with a greater appreciation of what we have. We find our life by giving it up. It all comes back to letting go.

Letting go sounds risky. We envision ourselves dangling from a window. We fear that if we loosen our grip we'll hit bottom and never bounce back. In truth, when we muster the courage to drop our defenses, we fall to a place of safety. The needy, guarded person we imagine ourselves to be surrenders to the confident, expansive, and fully satisfied One we really are.

That's why caring for the dying is such a wonderful practice. Loving someone enough to give care for them moves us beyond our fears. The riveting intensity of the work pulls us into accepting our life as it is.

A death among family or friends opens a window on the core of reality. Old scars crack, and we see the ways we make ourselves suffer. Change becomes possible. We learn to rejoice in our life.

This is not the submissive "Thy will be done." It is the active embracing of "Thy will" as mine. Through the reality of our particular life we love all life. Love of life, rather than fear of death, heals us into the larger community of beings. We become whole by finding our place in the whole universe.

Caregiving is truly transformative. During my first year as a caregiver, I underwent a simple but profound change in outlook. Now, if the day ends with a beautiful sunset and I have a backache, I tend to pay more attention to the sunset than the backache!

This book grows out of my two years as a volunteer with the Zen Hospice Project in San Francisco. The Project's unique combination of Eastern and hospice philosophy has stirred extensive interest and inspired similar projects around the world. Headquartered in an elegantly restored Victorian kitty-corner from the San Francisco Zen Center, the Project recruits and trains volunteers to care for terminal patients in a twenty-eight-bed ward in the city-owned Laguna Honda Hospital and in a four-bed, homelike unit on the second floor of the hospice headquarters building itself.

This smaller unit, known as the Guest House, is where I began working five hours a week, doing everything from taking temperatures to taking out the trash, from wiping bottoms to washing dead bodies. It is, as they say, a complete practice. What I learned there forms the foundation for this book. I hope the lessons and methods will help all readers find greater wisdom and compassion through caring for a loved one who is dying.

It is said that in spiritual studies all is contained in the very first lesson. On a fall day in late 1992 I got my first lesson in hospice work. Fresh out of volunteer training, I arrived for my shift nervously expecting big things to happen. Training had stirred up strong feelings. Along with listening to lectures on pain and symptom management, family dynamics, massage therapy, and grief and bereavement, I had played the roles of patient and caregiver, explored my own death through guided meditation, and talked with actual dying people. It had been exhausting and scary, and now here I was.

I mounted the imposing front steps and pushed the bell. After a long delay the door swung open. I was welcomed and handed the following terse list of duties:

Trash out
Wastebaskets
Laundry
Diaper cart
Compost bucket
Water pitchers

Thus, on my first day, I learned that hospice work, like everything else, is mostly a matter of maintenance.

Not long after I started, one cool, gray Sunday morning, my care partner Anandi met me at the door with an ashen expression. She was talking into the portable phone, gently trying to get the message across that someone, a loved one, had died. I was new and didn't know the deceased, so I left Anandi in the hallway and went to put the kettle on.

After a while she joined me in the kitchen, and we sat in silence, sipping yellow chamomile tea from glass cups. At last she said with a sigh, "It's that you have to deal with all their feelings. . . ." She was dealing with hers. I went upstairs to meet the dead man.

He was lying on the bed in the bay window, bathed in soft, fog-filtered light. Completing the fragile, saintly tableau, Anandi had folded his graceful hands over a long-stemmed lavender rose. Seeing both man and flower emptied of life, I was overcome by the beauty of my own breath. Existence had never seemed so sweet. When the ambulance came, I held open the front door for the stretcher bearers wanting to shout into the street as they took his body away: Hey! This man was here and now he isn't! Hey—wake up!

In his poem "A Refusal to Mourn the Death, by Fire, of a Child in London," Dylan Thomas concludes that "after the first death, there is no other." Don't believe it. You can't get used to death, not if you're really alive. The first time gave me a jolt of awareness. Later, with the passing of patients with whom I'd become friends, death wasn't always such a positive experience. But then sometimes it was. There was no rule. Of the deaths I shared—and I use that term advisedly—each was unique in its impact.

As a new volunteer, meeting patients for the first time I'd wonder how I'd react to losing them. In time I learned to put aside expectations and just do the next thing to be done. Not only is this the best way to do the work, it's the best way to live. Centuries ago a teacher instructed his students with a famous dictum consisting of three words: "Only don't know." The bedside of the dying is a place where you only don't know over and over and over again.

During my first few weeks, an elderly Russian Jewish lady arrived who left me little time for reflecting on the deeper lessons of the work. Adele was a former midwestern clothier of some success dying of lung cancer and having a hard time admitting it. Made irritable by illness and by fear, she diverted herself by telling us how we weren't doing the job to her standards. Every now and then she'd goad us about our inadequacies with sharp little digs like "Maybe I'll go to the Mayo Clinic." She rattled me, the new volunteer, but Harriet, who headed up the Guest House staff, was tickled to have a woman of gumption around. Harriet got such genuine amusement out of Adele's performances that even Adele had to smile.

After a few weeks of receiving persistently good care and good-will, Adele began to relax. I first experienced the flowering of her better nature when I botched the job of making her bed. Having sheets changed can be painful for patients because it requires them to move ailing bodies. I was a novice, and I was clumsy in getting Adele out of bed. Even worse, I kept her huddled on the sofa far too long because I couldn't get the sheets tucked in properly, and her aging husband had to help me. Adele bore it all with a patient look that said I was not only forgiven but also appreciated. It was as good a reward as I've ever gotten.

As Adele began losing strength, her cocky repartee gave way to long periods of silence. But the less she talked, the more I felt for her. There was a depth and intensity in her eyes that spoke of tremendous long-suffering. She discovered how to settle down on it, finding a safe, calm place where she could rest silently for hours. But when she did speak, she still spoke frankly.

One Sunday in February when her husband was ill, I sat with Adele reading a book while holding her hand. Bathed in gray winter light, the room was as quiet as a cathedral. After a while she asked me what I was reading. "A book of meditations," I replied. "So you're one of those, too," she said, turning away with a look of disgust. I loved her for saying that.

Four days later, when I was in the meditation hall, an inexplicable anguish overcame me. When I got home there was a message: Adele had died peacefully at 6:40 A.M. It was almost exactly the moment I felt that overwhelming sadness.

Later I learned she had kept her wit sharp to the end. Apparently the person caring for her had noticed that Adele's skin felt cool to the touch and had said something to her about it. "Of course I'm cold," she snapped back. "I'm almost dead!" Not many breaths more and she was. Truthful to the end.

In working with the dying the only constant is change. By this time we had David Wells, and he was very demanding. Tall, gangly, gaunt, often moody, manipulative, and highly theatrical, David favored black clothes and dramatic gestures. Hospice work is so pressing and practical—changing diapers, making meals, administering pain pills—we didn't have much time for his flamboyance. But we did take his talk of suicide seriously. David did not handle pain well. As I helped him ease his aching body into the bathtub, he was full of fear and remorse. "I had another life," he said. "It wasn't like this."

Although David worked us hard with his moods and complaints, his unceasing effort to experience himself fully in the last days of his life commanded our total respect. He was putting out a personal newsletter, holding late-night salons with his friends, and every now and then tottering down the hallway to console other patients. In time, David underwent a stunning transformation. His relentless self-searching had found expression in art. The walls of his room were covered with wavy, pastel drawings of crosses, flowers, humanoid figures, abstract designs. He sat at his window for hours, a sketch pad on his knees, his eyes illuminated by interior light.

One day he asked my opinion about his strange, psychically driven drawings. I rather liked what he was working on. There was something both familiar and weirdly intriguing about the bulbous "Mr. Tomato Man," the tooth-shaped, faintly Asian "Chang," and the big-eared "Mr. Mousy." We talked about colors, about symbolism, about the names that he'd given his characters. I suggested that he do a comic strip, but he said he didn't have the energy. That's when it hit me: David was much weaker now; he wouldn't last much longer. When my shift was over, I turned back at the door to have a look at him. He blessed me with a deep smile that said he was ready to die. I wasn't ready to let him. But he did anyway.

Soon after that, cooling winds brought relief from the unusual summer hot spell that had kept San Francisco restless. Fog peered down from the top of the Page Street hill as I walked to the hospice. Inside the mood matched the weather. The new group of patients was cool and introspective. Time and people passed by, leaving so little. The past, says the poet William Matthews, is "the little we remember." I couldn't remember the names of all those who had died in the hospice. It was troubling. If I couldn't remember them, were they here? Was I?

The caregiver's path is difficult. Experiencing our mortality through the death of another evokes troubling thoughts and feelings, but the pain, fear, and loss serve to wake us from our slumber. Death demands that we question our lives. Caregiving offers as the answer an unbounded experience of being. The light of the dying reveals our greatest wealth to be life as it is. Thus the paradox: Giving care to the dying gives new life to us. Having witnessed this in myself and others, I sometimes wonder if it's not the "mission" of the dying to illumine those they leave behind and thus help humans survive as a species.

HOW THIS BOOK IS ORGANIZED

The vast truths of caring for the dying express themselves in a multitude of details. To keep the caregiver from getting overwhelmed, *At Home with Dying* contains a comprehensive index and descriptive chapter subheadings. Sources are fully noted at the end of the book.

Although the work is detailed, we do it best when we approach it in the right frame of mind. The three sections of *At Home with*

Dying are grouped around the mind-set appropriate to each section's tasks.

The first section, "Beginner's Mind," introduces the work and encourages a willingness to approach it with a mind emptied of expectations. The second, "Caregiver's Mind," is the practical heart of the book. It describes in detail the essential bedside practices and explains how to do them with compassion and awareness. Each chapter in this section concludes with a step-by-step description of a practical technique, or Home Skill. The third section, "Inquiring Mind," reflects on death's lessons for the living. The Appendix includes useful reference and referral information, and the book ends with suggestions for further reading.

I

Beginner's Mind

In the beginner's mind there are many possibilities, but in the expert's there are few.

—Shunryu Suzuki-roshi

One

Why You Should Help
Your Loved One Die at Home

Because you have a tender heart.
Because it is asked of you.
Because you are afraid.
Because you can make a difference.

M OST AMERICANS—87 percent, according to a Gallup poll—would rather die at home, surrounded by friends and familiar possessions.[1] Instead, most of us die in a hospital. What is this like?

It's painful and expensive, according to a study that made headlines in late 1995.[2] The two-phase study, spanning five teaching hospitals and 9,100 patients over four years, was the most extensive investigation ever conducted into dying in an American hospital. The disturbing results rocked the public and brought down a storm of criticism on the medical profession.

According to the study, known by the acronym SUPPORT, doctors routinely allowed death to be unnecessarily prolonged and painful. People died isolated from their loved ones and invaded by feeding tubes or hooked up to machines that kept them alive *against their wishes*. As a consequence, nearly a third of the patients and their families spent all or most of their savings on vain and unwanted medical procedures that could not prevent the inevitable.

Even worse, when an attempt was made in the second phase of

the study to awaken doctors and hospitals to the cruel futility of these practices, absolutely nothing changed. Despite the intervention of special nurse-advocates, almost the same numbers of dying patients were found to be isolated in intensive care units, allowed to endure untreated pain, and aggressively kept alive against their wishes. Not only is the American system of hospital-based terminal care out of touch with humanity, it is out of control.

And that, my friend, is where you come in. By choosing to be a caregiver, you can help someone dear to you die at home, free from unwanted medical interventions, relieved of as much pain as possible, and warmed by the sun of your loving attention.

That may sound like a tall order. In the midst of a hurried life, who has the time and stamina to look after a dying person? How can our loved ones' many needs be met? What about managing the pain? And isn't special training required?

Yes, the work can be demanding. Like home cooking, helping a loved one die at home takes a little extra effort. There are new things to learn about the human body and the disease process, and about medicines and their side effects. You'll learn practical nursing skills and become familiar with health care professionals and institutions and with the legal side of dying.

And you'll learn new things about yourself. The big discovery is that you already have what it takes.

Becoming caregivers does not require new strengths. It is a matter of recognizing the strengths we already have. Humans are born to help each other; this is our most fulfilling role. When we take care of others, they take care of us by offering an opportunity to affirm our own best instincts. Over time we come to recognize our natural capacity to listen and to love, and we are able to embrace this inherent goodness and live it more fully. Taking care of the dying is demanding work, but we should approach it with confidence and hope because it carries within it the power to genuinely transform us.

There is a saying: "When the student is ready, the teacher appears." Are you ready to let your dying loved one be your teacher?

I belong to one of the several generations of Americans for whom death has been a stranger hidden away in hospitals and funeral homes. When it finally arrived at my door, the response was fear and embarrassment. What to say? What to do?

It's instinctual for living beings to pull away from death. Even many species of animals shun their own dead. Wise societies compensate by developing rituals and practices to bring death into consciousness so the fear can be dissipated. In this way living unfolds in a healthy relationship with dying. Tibetans make awareness of death the cornerstone of their entire culture. Ours goes to the opposite extreme.

Much has been written about America's chronic denial of death. Our society sees death as tragic, horrible, unlawful, unwanted, or comic, but never normal and necessary. In America, observes the medical ethicist Daniel Callahan, we see death as almost a sin.[3] The great wealth and opportunity of this country seem to have fostered the notion that we should be even more than we can be—immortal.

The medical establishment feeds the myth. "For research medicine there are no tolerable causes of death," writes Callahan. Research medicine prolonged life by eradicating common infectious diseases and developing effective accident treatments, but it also prolonged the process of dying. Terminal patients suffering from progressive conditions such as cancer, heart disease, and diabetes now decline over a matter of years rather than months. With new treatments, AIDS, too, has been added to the list of long-term illnesses. In the context of the American system of dying, extending the end of our lives has a side effect: most dying people now spend some eighty days in a hospital or nursing home. If the SUPPORT researchers are right, it's not a good way to go. What's the alternative?

Although 80 percent of Americans now die sequestered in hospitals, it wasn't always so. At the turn of the century most of us died at home. Death was more of an expected family and community event that touched and involved everyone. Over the last two decades a gentle grassroots revolution in terminal care has brought back a more homelike, less frantic kind of dying. In the same year the SUPPORT findings made public the widespread hospital mistreatment of the dying, some 375,000 Americans opted to complete their lives in hospices. More than 75 percent of these hospice clients had cancer; most of the rest had AIDS, heart disease, and long-term illnesses like Lou Gehrig's disease.

THE HOSPICE MODEL OF HOME CARE

Hospice is many things, but first of all it is a philosophy. Hospice believes that dying is not a defeat but rather a natural part of human life. And because death has to happen, hospice allows it to happen with maximum respect for each person's inherent worth and with reverence for the process. The hospice return to home death tradition brings with it a high level of consciousness.

Hospice originated in Christian Rome and developed throughout the Middle Ages as a church-based network of resting places for people in transition: travelers, the sick, and the dying. In America hospice is less often a place than a program of care. Ninety percent of hospice care is carried out at home.

This is an important point that is often overlooked. People tend to think of hospice as a hospital for the dying, and sometimes it is. A hospice can be a freestanding structure, or it can be a hospital ward. But most of the time hospice happens at home. The dying person stays at home or with family or friends and receives care from a team put together by a visiting nurse or home health agency.

The home care team typically includes both professional and nonprofessional members. There is a nurse, a social worker, a home health aide, and a spiritual counselor, all working in consultation with a physician. And there are volunteers who help primary caregivers with everything from baby-sitting to grocery shopping.

Remember the term *primary caregiver*. You'll see it often in this book. Home care is a team effort, and extensive support services are available, but the around-the-clock responsibility of ensuring that the dying person gets fed, cleaned, and comforted usually falls on a single committed family member, lover, or friend.

This is how home care is usually organized:

✦ One or two people are the primary caregivers, who take charge of the bedside work. They either do it themselves or see that it gets done by others.

✦ Hospice professionals provide technical advice and assistance.

✦ Friends and loved ones form a wider caregiving circle that supports both the patient and the primary caregivers.

If you think the primary caregiver might be you, rest easy. Caregiving is a difficult path, but with the help of home care professionals you won't walk it alone. When you get involved with a dying loved one, they get involved with you.

The staff will develop a detailed care plan specific to your loved one's condition. To help you implement the plan, the home care nurse will come by two or three times a week for an hour or two to see how both patient and family are doing. The visiting nurse and the home health aide will tutor you in bedside techniques and help you obtain any specialized equipment; the social worker will walk you through the paperwork that makes federal and state aid possible; counselors will be there for your pain and strain; and volunteers will want nothing more than to put themselves at your service. The home team is your team, too, and its members are there to help you through the hard times.

The first popular misconception about hospice is that it's a place, like a hospital. In America it's usually a program rather than a place.

Another common misconception is that hospice is a place where people go to *die*. In fact, it is all about life, not death. A hospice program does not hasten death; it adds life to someone's last days. For staff and volunteers the work is one of meeting each person wherever he or she is and accompanying the person all the way to the end.

"We need to see patients and their pain at the deepest level," says Dr. Derek Kerr, attending physician at Laguna Honda Hospice in San Francisco. "When we do this they feel seen, they feel understood, and they experience trust."

The result can be very beautiful. Many times I've seen family and friends come away from a deathbed radiant with joy and deeply grateful for the kind of acceptance that home care makes possible.

HOSPICE IN AMERICA

Hospice is a national and international movement that began in London and came to the United States in 1974. There are now 2,700 programs in fifty states and Puerto Rico, and these programs are well integrated into the health care system. Health departments certify them in all states. Services are covered under most public and private health plans, including Medicare. For a person to qualify, a doctor must certify that death is likely within six months. Most hospices will accept those who can't pay, using donated funds to cover the cost.

The American hospice community of some 25,000 paid professionals and 100,000 volunteers shares a strong sense of mission and a clear consensus on the fundamentals. These are:

✦ *Holistic care.* Hospice addresses as many dimensions of the patient as possible, blends lay and professional caregivers, considers the quality of caregiving to be as important as medication, and respects the unique integrity of the way each person dies.

✦ *Effective pain management.* Hospice leads the health care professions in discovering new and better ways to treat pain in all its aspects. Physical, mental, and spiritual pain are relieved through medication, counseling, and loving care.

✦ *Receptivity to death.* Patients are told they are going to die, death is considered normal, and the search for meaning is seen as part of the process. Hospice is much more than "making the best of a bad situation."

✦ *Involvement of family and friends.* Staff and volunteers are trained to help family, friends, and patient come together to make important decisions, maintain a high level of care, and encourage a dying process that enriches the lives of all.

✦ *Healthy grieving.* Hospice acknowledges the need for bereavement. Staff supports the patient, family, and friends in their grief.

✦ *Minimal intervention.* Hospice medically treats only conditions that improve the quality of life. As few as possible laboratory tests are performed, and intravenous antibiotics are almost never used. Aggressive treatments are used when they will reduce pain. These treatments may include feedings, radiation, surgery, and chemotherapy.

✦ *Health care professionals in a support position.* The most important people in the dying process are the patient and the caregivers—not doctors, nurses, or other health care professionals.

In the midst of the impersonal machine that health care has become, hospice is an enlightened development. Hospice is an idea whose time has come. Yet most Americans still die in a hospital. Why?

THE OSTRICH MODEL OF DYING

Death is pretty scary, especially in America. Our culture provides so little useful advice about death that when it approaches we tend to stick our heads in the sand like ostriches.

Avoidance can have painful consequences. Dying fearful and

mute in a hospital is not a good way to go. The SUPPORT researchers found that terminally ill patients who failed to communicate their views about resuscitation, feeding tubes, and other invasive medical procedures too often met a bitter end.

The stark vision of dying in an impersonal hospital stuck full of tubes and attended by strangers haunts many elderly and dying people. They fear hospitals almost as much as they fear death, but they don't know the hospice alternative or understand its difference. How fortunate are those who learn that death can be greeted gracefully with the assistance of a hospice program and its many resources.

Hospice home care is wonderful, but enrolling in a program can be a difficult decision. The course of many diseases makes it hard for doctors to predict with accuracy how long a terminally ill person has to live, and no one wants to commit prematurely to the idea of actively dying.

Determining when to go on moving toward life and when to accept death as inevitable can be an excruciating dilemma that involves loved ones and friends. Anyone for whom death is a possibility and not a certainty can use the help of trustworthy counselors.

If your loved one hovers on this troubling threshold, hospice professionals can help determine if it's appropriate to continue aggressive efforts to "beat" the disease or if it's time to stop. Remember that anyone who shows signs of recovery can be discharged from a hospice program. Such dropouts aren't unusual. Should they need to reenter, Medicare and most private insurance will provide coverage.

Sometimes the resistance originates with the patient's doctor. A doctor's prognosis of six months or less to live is required to enroll in most hospice programs, but doctors tend to push dying people to "go down fighting." And in our society, where the initials M.D. carry godlike authority, it's hard for an ailing person to summon up the strength to overrule this opinion.

One of the most pressing issues in the hospice movement is how to encourage doctors to refer patients earlier and more often. The problem has its origin in the medical school curriculum. Only five of the 126 medical schools in the United States offer a separate required course on the care of the dying.[4]

Without adequate training, doctors may look down on a hospice referral as a confession of failure to keep death at bay. Or they may be unaware just how much hospice can help. If you think your loved one's doctor could benefit from having more information about hospice, you might tactfully suggest a toll-free call to the **National Hospice Helpline, 1-800-658-8898**.

The idea of entering a home care program does not have to originate with a physician. The dying person and family and friends are always free to explore the options with anyone whose advice and expertise are valued. Ultimately the decision to enroll belongs, by law, to the patient.

CHOOSING HOME CARE

It would be unfair and inaccurate to blame doctors for America's death-denying culture. If medical science lacks a sense of limits, that's because we expect too much of it. Science has conquered so many diseases we've come to think it's invincible. It isn't.

Science can give us longer lives, but it can't give us immortality. The irony is that by prolonging our life, science has actually prolonged our dying. Now instead of passing away suddenly we tend to die progressively, over many months or years.

This profound shift has not been fully absorbed into our society. We still tend to think of death as sudden, perhaps because that's the way we'd like it to be. "I want to live fast, love hard, die young, and leave a beautiful memory," sang country music's Faron Young. But for most of us dying will take place late in life and over a long period of time. And that's good, because we have not only more life but also more options for how it will end.

Knowing in advance that death is coming, we can choose how to meet it. We can specify the medical treatments we want and don't want. We can decide how much support we're willing to seek from friends and family. We can ensure that our cultural, religious, and spiritual beliefs will be respected. And we can choose whether we want to die in a hospital or at home, assisted by hospice.

In short, people who have a terminal illness now have a lot to say about their dying. Instead, all too often, they say nothing. How could it be otherwise in a society where the subject of death is taboo? Fewer than one in five Americans will even confess to thinking about death in a serious way, according to a Gallup poll.[5] Until society adopts a more wholesome, open view of death, dying people will continue to resist making conscious choices.

If you are the one who should persuade your dying loved one to consider home care, find a way to do it gently, but do it. Do it now.

CHOOSING TO BE A CAREGIVER

Home care is now widely available in America. The dying have a wonderful option to choose, and this poses choices as well for family members, loved ones, and friends. Home care requires caregivers. Are you one?

There's no need to rush a decision. Bring family and close friends into the discussion. These are the people who will form the center of your loved one's **support group.**

The support group sustains the patient, the primary caregiver, and its own members. Group members are responsible for specific tasks (cleaning, providing fresh flowers, getting prescriptions) carried out under the coordination of the primary caregiver. A **phone tree** keeps the support group connected in case of emergency. The Home Skill section at the end of Chapter 5 explains how to form a support group.

Regular support group meetings give members a chance to share their experiences, their feelings, and their perceptions of the patient's needs. These discussions are an excellent forum for raising consciousness about the spiritual nature of caregiving work. It may be helpful to invite a cleric, counselor, or spiritual teacher and to connect with other volunteers providing terminal care and invite them to share their experiences. In the spiritual practice of taking care of the dying, the support group can be the spiritual community should you choose to take on this challenging job.

It can be "plain hard slogging without much uplift," writes my e-mail pen pal Douglas Penick. Having just shepherded a friend through a difficult dying, Penick wanted me to mention "how sometimes, dying people are quite unpleasant, hard to take, utterly demanding, capricious, ungrateful, all around difficult, provide no C-chord ending at their final demise, and leave their friends and family in considerable disarray."

In assessing your resources, be as realistic as possible—caring for the dying is as real as it gets. Keeping a bedridden person fed, cleaned, turned, and free from bedsores is an around-the-clock responsibility requiring a full circle of support.

At the center of the circle is the **primary caregiver**. This complex role combines nurse, doctor, therapist, teacher, social secretary, spiritual counselor, and intimate companion. Add full- or part-time employment plus the pressures of managing a household and tending to other family and social demands and the load is large.

Still, caregiving work is essentially simple. Remember that hospice doesn't try to cure illness or hasten death. Its goal is to provide the deepest possible companionship because no one should die feeling abandoned. Fleet Maull, who founded the National Prison Hospice Association, says even the most hardened criminals want someone near them at the end. And that's where you, the caregiver, come in.

Caregiving is all about accompaniment. When you choose to take care of a dying person, you accompany that person all the way to the end. It can be a rocky road. Caring for a dying loved one has a special intensity. Even medical professionals find their detachment fails them when they work with a partner, friend, or relative.

Caregiving stretches our physical and emotional limits, but the biggest challenge is change. This is a time of constantly restructuring our relationships with our loved ones. What works well one day is inappropriate the next because the dying person's rapidly changing mind and body are continually creating new circumstances. We respond by keeping open a loving and compassionate space in which our patients can participate as much as possible in making the choices that affect them.

Some choices are best made by the dying person, such as when to let go of the hope of recovery. (The doctor makes the death prognosis; the patient decides when to believe it.) Others may be made jointly by patient and caregiver, such as deciding when it is necessary for the patient to leave home and move to a hospice. And then there are the many small decisions made much larger by the presence of death. Is it possible to take your patient out for a walk, or has she become too weak? Is it time to put a commode in his room, thus letting it be publicly known that he has become too weak to get to the toilet?

The many questions in caregiving find their answers in practical reality. The work is basically helpful and pragmatic, and this keeps us grounded. When emotions run high, we don't get lost in the drama because there's always another ordinary thing to do. "After the ecstasy, the laundry" is the way one volunteer put it.

PAIN MANAGEMENT

Before we begin caregiving, fear may loom as the worst part of the experience. Spending long hours with someone who is dying, especially someone dying in one's own home, can feel like a personal threat. And this fear can trigger others.

What will the neighbors think about having a dying person next door? Will we be able to perform perineal (genital area) care or cope with incontinence? What if my loved one suffers cognitive impairment and "loses his mind"? What if she asks me to aid her in suicide?

Given the way our society distances us from death, these are very normal and natural responses. Thousands of Americans have begun hospice caregiving with similar fears and then seen these fears dissipate in the course of doing the work.

Living with a loved one's dying lets us be intimate with our own fears of dying and thus achieve greater freedom from them. There is daring, and even danger, on the hospice path to wisdom, and the heart responds with a courage that comes from compassion.

Compassion itself can give rise to fears of being unable to relieve pain. By now you may have seen your loved one in pain, or at least breathing with difficulty, and the experience may have caused you anxiety. How will you feel as the illness gets worse? Will the pain get out of control?

As shown by numerous studies of both AIDS and cancer patients, pain is a serious issue for the dying. Some 70 to 90 percent of people with advanced cancer have, at some point, severe, unrelenting physical and psychological pain that can interfere with their sleep, their daily activities, and their relationships with others.[6]

That's the bad news. The good news is that 90 percent of cancer pain can be effectively relieved. The breakthrough discovery on controlling pain wasn't achieved by highly funded teams of medical researchers but by the extraordinary woman who founded the modern hospice movement, Dr. Cicely Saunders.

At her London hospice Dr. Saunders discarded conventional notions of pain management based on symptom treatment. She started administering much higher drug dosages that improved the quality of life for the dying without "snowing" them under. The critical factor was maintaining good communication between patient and staff. She also incorporated counseling and other therapies into her holistic approach.

That was in the mid-1960s. When the hospice movement spread to the United States a few years later, it brought Dr. Saunders's methods of pain management with it. Her enlightened approach was thoroughly incorporated by American hospice doctors and nurses. It's now standard to expect that in most cases a dying person's pain can be made entirely manageable. When pain occurs, you will have a way to help with it.

Although you have every reason to trust hospice home care professionals to reduce your loved one's pain to an acceptable level, you can't expect the same from a hospital. Hospital doctors, nurses, and even cancer specialists routinely undermedicate patients with life-threatening illness. This is confirmed by several studies. In one, 42 percent of physicians were found to let several thousand cancer patients suffer unnecessary pain.[7] Obviously hospital staff have access to the same medications as hospice staff. Why don't they use them?

Dr. Joanne Lynn, who codirected the SUPPORT research, believes doctors allow people to suffer pain in dying because they don't see their patients' condition as terminal soon enough. "Your pain doesn't count for much if you are going to get better and go home," she told an interviewer. "We never step back and say, 'Wait a minute. This is how a person is living.'"[8]

Home care is all about living, not dying. Its staff are completely committed to relieving any pain that might prevent a dying person from living her last days fully. By helping your friend or loved one die in a home care program rather than in a hospital, you are making it possible for her to obtain the best pain treatment possible.

As a caregiver, you will be a critical link for the flow of information about your loved one's response to the hospice pain management plan. Your observations recorded in the **Patient Log** (see the Home Skill section at the end of Chapter 7) will provide vital data for determining and revising the proper drugs and dosages.

CAREGIVING AS OPPORTUNITY

We approach caregiving thinking it is something we do for other people. Over time we discover that it is also something we do for ourselves. The dying person's great need for help teaches us—often against our will—how to give it. Caregiving is not a duty but an opportunity.

In California, where I live, the human potential movement of the 1970s has evolved into a full-fledged nontraditional religious revival. Tens of thousands of people flock to classes, workshops, retreats, seminars, and conferences offered by a host of teachers, shamans, therapists, and gurus. The booming inner-growth industry is certainly producing better health and a brighter outlook, but are people really changing *inside?*

Fundamental change is very difficult. There's an old saying that "character is destiny," the kind of person each of us is determines how our lives develop. Our personalities have such a strong grip on us that we tend to remain entrenched in habitual ways unless something radical jolts us out of the rut.

Going through a divorce can do it, or losing a job, or suffering a disabling injury, or hitting rock bottom in a destructive addiction. For Dannion Brinkley, author of the best-selling book *Saved by the Light*, lightning did it.

Brinkley was enjoying his macho life as a Marine counterinsurgency expert who went around blowing things up when a bolt of lightning hit him in the neck. The charge shot down his spine, welded the nails of the heels of his shoes to the nails in the floor, and knocked him out of his shoes and into the air. He came crashing down, bending the bed frame and leaving him clinically dead for twenty-eight minutes. During this time something extraordinary happened.

The way Brinkley tells it, he had a perception of leaving his body and merging into a gentle blue-gray mist. This began a journey of consciousness on which he met wondrous beings who infused him with the conviction that the law of human life is to love thy neighbor as thyself. "It's wild when you start to realize that there's a type of interwoven fabric between us and everyone else," he told an interviewer.[9]

After returning to his body and to consciousness, Brinkley put his new insight to work. The macho Marine became a hospice and nursing home volunteer. By mid-1995 he had assisted some 149 people in their dying. His motto is, "If you are terminal and you're afraid of dying, you can come to me, and I listen."

So the truth, like home care, is really very simple—it's the Golden Rule. And putting this truth into action is no big deal either. You just keep your ears open and when somebody needs help, you respond. Forget the classes, workshops, teachers, therapists, gurus, retreats, seminars, conferences, and techniques. Just listen and respond. That's the truth, that's it.

Not so fast, I hear you saying. I may know the truth, but that doesn't mean I know how to live it. How do I make the truth *me?*

Dannion Brinkley's way can't be easily followed. The odds of becoming enlightened by a bolt from the blue are pretty slim. Most of us have to make a conscious effort. The catch-22 is that we can't achieve spiritual growth until we've grown up enough to realize that it takes hard work.

From this perspective caregiving is not just getting the job done but learning from its stress and difficulty. That may sound like self-centeredness, but it is actually the most effective approach. If you make "getting back to normal" your standard, caregiving will utterly exhaust you. Embark on a voyage of self-discovery and you'll find yourself buoyed up by the work. If you're ready for a challenge big enough to change you, welcome to home care.

HOW WE CHANGE

Caregiving's uncertainty is what gives the work such transformative power. To change we have to be willing to be knocked off center. There is a sense of surrender, of feeling inadequate, that teaches us how fully adequate we are.

Listen to these wise words Larry Hjort, an AIDS caregiver who himself has AIDS, told Charles Garfield, founder of San Francisco's Shanti Project: "Inadequacy is a human invention, it's a judgment we make. It doesn't really exist. In fact everyone is perfectly adequate. There are just some impossible situations."[10]

Caring for a dying person is an impossible situation that can jolt us into remembering who we really are. The work is so compelling it can yank us out of our expectations and inject us into the present. And this is where we find our spiritual home. Like Dannion Brinkley's near-death experience, caregiving brings home the truth that we are deeply connected with each other. When we encounter this truth, the very earth slips away. (It's "wild," says Brinkley.) We see our patients as ourselves, and we discover that no real difference exists between us and others.

It's a truth that can rock us. If we and our loved ones are the same, then their deaths are ours. Seeing the ways they change, the challenges they must overcome, we are compelled to recognize that their experience will also be ours. Their shock, resistance, and—finally—acceptance will be our process, too.

It's a process that is already present. In every moment of life we resist or accept what comes up. Working with a dying person lets us recognize that dying is not separate from living. By showing us the unity of living and dying, hospice caregiving gives us the practical training in life that our culture does not. Adapting to our own mortality, we embrace life as it is. Caregiving is all about life.

CAREGIVING AS PRACTICE

Caregiving as a method of achieving inner change is illustrated by this teaching story passed down from China. It seems that a monk was wandering in a forest littered with leaves. Struck by the vast disorder, the monk leaned down and picked up a leaf, saying, "This is one less leaf lying on the forest floor."

Many times I've finished my shift feeling like nothing more than a keeper of the karmic forest, but these efforts to tidy up the falling timbers were not in vain. They changed both me and the situation. In the movies death is announced when the doctor folds his arms and says, "Nothing more can be done." In hospice caregiving, something more can always be done. And the act of doing changes the doer because taking care of the dying is fundamentally a spiritual practice.

The word *practice* tends to evoke memories of childhood duty. We look back on long hours at the piano or learning how to throw a fastball or turn a not-too-wobbly pirouette. The drill wasn't much fun, which is why a lot of reluctant young pianists—including me— never got much beyond "Clair de Lune." But others stuck with it and achieved mastery.

Through practice it's possible to take a big goal, like winning the Little League championship or becoming a prima ballerina, and break it down into small repetitive actions that we can do until we get it right. A *New Yorker* cartoon a few years back showed a bushy-haired musician with a violin case telling a tourist how to get to Carnegie Hall: "Practice, practice, practice."

Caregiving has two things in common with this tedious "practice makes perfect." First, taking care of a dying person is composed largely of small, ordinary actions done so often they can become quite tiring. Day after day we help our loved ones eat, sleep, take pills, drink water, use the toilet, and stay clean and free from bedsores. Second, the work can lead to bigger things because dying amplifies ordinary tasks.

A dying person is fragile in every sense, and the caregiver must summon up large amounts of emotional, and sometimes physical, stamina to meet the many needs. It is precisely the demanding intensity of the work that gives it its transformative power.

Eihei Dogen, the great twelfth-century master, wrote that "everyday mind opens the gate of the inner chamber."[11] Feed a dying person one spoonful at a time and you'll get an insight into what Dogen meant. There's a heightened concentration that can open the heart to a deep, inner stillness. Absorbed in our caregiving, we forget who we are supposed to be—and we become who we really are.

This luminous forgetfulness can be our natural resting place if we don't strive too hard to achieve it. Caregiving takes us to our spiritual destination when we give up hope of getting there, because caregiving is aimed not at results but at process. We measure success by what we put into the work rather than by what we get out of it.

In this respect caregiving is radically different from a practice that leads to learning new skills. Suzuki-roshi said we meditate not to acquire something special but to express our true nature, and caregiving is the same. The purpose is not to master a technique but to master our capacity to be ourselves. Deeply embracing our loved ones just as they are opens the way for us to embrace who *we* are.

Caregiving is a path, and we make the way by walking it. One summer in my youth I worked on a trail crew repairing a steep part of the John Muir Trail that runs along California's Sierra Nevada Range. The trail was well marked on Geological Survey maps, but in the high country, where we were, snow and rock slides had made a mockery of the maps. We spent two months grunting and dynamiting a slender trail through the granite maze. It was shoulder-to-boulder work, and half the time we weren't sure where we were headed. All we could do was take it one big rock at a time until we got there. And we did.

Caregiving is transformative work, but that doesn't mean everyone should do it. If, after reading this chapter, you don't feel you have the personal or practical resources to take on caregiving at this time, please don't. Acknowledging limits shows wisdom, not weakness. Having reached a well-founded decision, you will be less likely to suffer from guilty second thoughts about what you should have done.

Whether or not we choose to be caregivers, the goal is the same. In the end, after our loved ones' passing, we want to grieve their loss—and not the thought that we didn't do all we could. When we do our best, there are no mistakes. In caring for a dying loved one, the best of intentions is good enough.

Two

Spiritual Care Is Nothing Special

First, do no harm.
—Hippocrates

THE AMERICAN HOSPICE MOVEMENT is growing rapidly. Given that hospice can provide a higher quality of long-term care than a hospital at half the cost, the rapid growth is not surprising, but with the expansion of the business of hospice, its spiritual origins should not be forgotten.

Hospice has deep roots in the spiritual traditions of both the West and the East. Shakyamuni Buddha instructed his followers to attend to the suffering of others. Five centuries later Jesus preached the same message. Both practiced what they preached by directly caring for the sick and dying.

During the Middle Ages, Christian hospice evolved into a highly organized pursuit. Blessed Gerard, a twelfth-century Benedictine monk, founded his Knights Hospitallers on the principle that providing hospitality was a path to spiritual perfection. Guests knocking at the door of the hospice were knocking at the door of the hospice worker's heart. "Hail, Guest," says an ancient inscription on a wall at Assisi. "Not only the door but the heart of my owner lies open to you."

In the statutes of Gerard's order, the work of opening the heart and abandoning self to serve others was called putting on the new man. Today we would call this inner work transformation. Many

Americans are willing to pay a steep price to seek it through a variety of psychological and spiritual therapies. Caregiving is an effective alternative. When we care for the dying, we care for ourselves.

SPIRITUAL CARE IS PRACTICAL CARE

Robert Pirsig begins *Zen and the Art of Motorcycle Maintenance* by observing how often "the truth knocks on the door and you say, 'go away, I'm looking for the truth.'"[1] In caring for a dying person, the deepest truths are unavoidable. We encounter them, as the adage instructs, by "taking one step off a hundred-foot pole."

It doesn't really matter whether we take that step and fall flat on our faces or fly to the moon. The important thing is to get directly involved. We achieve spiritual growth by embracing our experience. We give spiritual care the same way.

Spiritual care sounds like something special, but every caregiving task, no matter how mundane, contains a spiritual component when we do it wisely and from the heart. Working from the heart is sharing love; working wisely is doing the appropriate thing.

Dale Borglum, of the Living/Dying Project in Marin County, California, holds up as a model for spiritual care the volunteer who would climb into bed with her dying client so together they could eat chocolate ice cream and play with his teddy bear. Hers was a wonderfully wise and heartfelt spiritual care that was perfectly crafted for her friend.

A negative example comes from Douglas Penick, who has cared for several dying people. He says caregiving is "just heart and whatever it takes to bring that to bear." Unfortunately, some people don't seem to know this. Douglas writes, "When my grandmother was dying, a rather mealy-mouthed minister came by and offered to pray with her. 'I'd much prefer it if you told me a joke,' said she. But, as she told me later with considerable irritation, he didn't know any."

When it comes to spiritual care, one size doesn't fit all. Within the suffering, unpredictability, and uniqueness of each death are tasks tailored to that dying person. Our work is to help our loved ones meet their own particular set of challenges, because there are as many ways of dying as there are ways of living.

HOW WE DIE—A SCENARIO

Most of the words used to describe death evoke dramatic images of struggle: we succumb; we expire; we perish. But living out the last days of a long-term illness is a matter more of coping than of fighting. Imagine the following:

Your doctor just called. The lab tests are back. He says you've lost your long battle with cancer; only three months remain. Numb with shock and exhausted by disease you throw yourself down in bed. Days later the shock has worn off but you're terribly tired and filled with a longing to live. Now you know you'll never get well. You feel totally rotten, and nothing lifts the malaise. Favorite foods taste like chalk. Books and movies don't stop your mind from spinning.

A week goes by. You think you want visitors, but when friends drop in you're too angry to have them around. And yet more and more help is needed because you have so little strength. Even making a cup of tea is a grueling ordeal. Your loss of control is profound. You see your future slipping away; you can't always get to the bathroom in time. When your sister asks you to move in with her, you reluctantly agree. Your sister and her husband set you up in a lovely, well-lighted room. You are grateful to have their support, but you miss your own home.

Friends come by to visit you in your new residence. You welcome those who don't give advice and endure those with fear in their faces. As the weeks grind on, you get fewer visitors. While your sister and her husband are at work, you spend long hours alone with your thoughts. Faced with the prospect of dying, you search for the meaning of your life, but you have limited energy for self-exploration.

Pain hovers at the edge of awareness. Morphine makes the pain go away but causes constipation. The hospice nurse tries several laxatives before she finds one that works. Then you have a diarrhea attack. You are so weak that your sister and her husband must help you get out of bed and use the commode. They are kind, but you hate being so dependent. So you try to get up on your own and have a bad fall that leaves you bruised and depressed.

You can see the deep concern in the faces of friends and family. A growing feeling of love in your heart makes you want to comfort those around you. You look forward to the moments when your sister has time to sit and hold hands while you talk over old memories. With your sister's encouragement you manage to write a few short letters to friends and relatives you haven't seen in years. Some of them call back. You enjoy hearing from them; it makes you feel complete. But you also like quietly sorting through your life in silence. More and more the silence seems like enough, for now and forever.

Two months pass. Your sister has taken a leave from her job to care for you, but you refuse most of her offers to make you more comfortable. Conversation becomes a burden as your mind turns inward to bring your memories and thoughts together with the certainty of impending death.

You want only to be lightly touched or left alone. You spend more and more time sleeping. You eat only a little soft food and sip liquids only occasionally. The pain that required medication is now nearly gone, and at times your body feels almost weightless.

When your eyes are closed, as they are much of the time, you hear others say you've "given up" and you feel their despair. You wish you could comfort your family and friends, but they've grown very distant.

By now your body is rapidly shutting down. You have lost control of your bladder and bowels. Swallowing is difficult. Your pulse is sluggish, and you are too weak to roll over in bed. Restless agitation causes you to pick at your clothes and your bedding. You feel hot and then cold. Your brain receives less and less oxygen, causing mental confusion. And there are chemical changes, too. You have strange dreams; you wake up in the night. Failing eyesight and impaired speech make it hard for you to discern what is happening. You feel better when your sister softly tells you who you are and the day and time. You ask her to leave the light on all night.

You know only a little life remains, but you have no sense of time. You drift on a cloud of consciousness. Sometimes you respond to others; sometimes you don't. You see brilliant, full-color visions. You sleep with your eyes and mouth open. Someone is always nearby, and you welcome the presence, but when family members arrive from far away some of them are crying, and this disturbs you. You wish you could help them, but you are unable to move or even speak. And it's OK.

Your heart beats to an uneven rhythm. Breathing becomes erratic and noisy. Phlegm is collecting in your lungs and rattling around in the back of your throat. Now and then someone, your sister perhaps, carefully cleans the spit from your mouth and coolly dampens your forehead, but you don't really need any help. Even when your breath seems to lapse you aren't bothered. You have no fear. You feel a radiant glow lifting your mind and your breath, and then at last they seem to merge and rise like a mist. It warms in the sun and is gone.

DYING AS HEALING

Is death necessarily bad? As a caregiver I know that dying certainly isn't. Wonderful things are possible during the dying process, because dying presents an opportunity to fully heal inner wounds.

This spiritual healing is self-healing. "My body is sick," one man told me two weeks before his death, "but I am my own doctor." He wasn't referring to getting rid of disease; he knew he was terminally ill. He was talking about rediscovering who he really was.

We tend to wall off the parts of our lives we don't like, but as Priest Paul Haller says, "We don't enter life on our terms; we enter on life's terms." We can never be at ease with ourselves until we take down the walls of denial and embrace our lives with nothing left out.

When we unite with our experience of being, we become Being itself. We hear the voice of God and recognize it as our own. I believe this happens with many, if not all, dying people. Dying is a purifying process tending toward the truth. At least that is my belief.

As caregivers we should never let our spiritual beliefs come between us and our loved ones' very real death. Dying people do not conform to any beliefs; they simply die the way they must. The best we can hope for is that our loved ones will die in the way that expresses their lives, because this way of dying expresses life itself.

Our role in aiding spiritual healing is one of support. We can help our loved ones be as true as possible to their process by assisting only when needed. Too much intervention can cause them to deny, control, and repress that which needs to surface and be resolved.

Keeping *our* beliefs in the background helps *them* bring theirs to the fore. Whether they are Christian, Muslim, Buddhist, Jewish, New Age, or secular humanist, our job is to support them in their spiritual inquiry.

The work of caring for a dying person may change, enrich, and fulfill our spiritual views, but we don't bring our spirituality to the bedside—we find it there. The higher insight of hospice is derived from experience, not belief. If a deathbed conversion takes place, it happens in our own heads. In taking care of a dying person, we are asked to learn to let go. And that means letting go of any special spiritual or religious agendas that might come between us and our patients.

Some New Age and Eastern teachings give explicit instructions for how to help a person die well. Much can be done to straighten out the twisted, traumatic American way of dying; getting rid of heavy-handed medical intervention would certainly make the passage easier. But in revising traditional views we should be careful about imposing new "spiritual" models. Do dying people really need a Himalayan guru or a meditation instructor or esoteric scriptures channeled from a distant star? I don't think so. What they need is our acceptance made real and complete through our loving presence.

GIVING SPIRITUAL CARE

A dying person will naturally have many deep questions, both spoken and unspoken. Why did this happen to me? How does it affect my belief in God? Can I hope for a miracle? What happens after death?

Caregivers shouldn't rush in with their own answers. Instead we can affirm the vital importance of the inquiry by listening with full attention and from the heart. We work to establish with them an intimate ground of mutual respect and trust.

The work is one of letting go of reactivity, resting in attentive silence, and just going with them where they go. We accept their way as if it were our own. Sitting and listening without judging and without reacting, noting what's said and what's left unsaid, we seek only to understand. This way of being helps *them* understand.

When we listen well we know the time to talk. If our loved ones seem to be having trouble framing their deepest thoughts, it may take priming the pump to get a flow of conversation going. The following questions can encourage spiritual inquiry. This list comes on good authority. It was put together by Linda Pratt Mukai, who had to answer many questions about her terminal cancer. These are the ones she wished she'd been asked:

✦ What do you think about your illness?

✦ Are you worried?

✦ Do you want to talk about it?

✦ Have you thought about what happens after death?[2]

All practical care is spiritual care when we do it with awareness, but there are specific ways we can use our awareness to help our loved ones express their spirit. Ritual and ceremony help create conditions for encouraging what needs to happen. Candles, incense (if the scent is acceptable), fresh flowers, music, artwork, and poetry invite a feeling of intimacy with deep beliefs.

Here are four steps toward opening a sacred, silent space that fosters spiritual healing.

✦ First, with our loved ones' permission, we listen to quiet music with them or read aloud their favorite poetry or scripture, or play a guided meditation tape, or silently pray or meditate or just sit together and enjoy the light and the air. Sometimes a sacred space springs into being in "secular" moments, when we're helping them bathe, for example, or giving a massage.

✦ Second, while sharing this space we quiet our chattering minds and center ourselves, using any method that grounds us in the quiet place within. My practice is breathing from the lower belly, as described in Chapter 6.

✦ Third, we invoke whatever divine image, or thought, or feeling gives us courage and hope. And we surrender to it. We simply let go of everything, especially the notion that we can "do something" for our loved ones. We just take a breath and let God run it. For this one moment we are willing to let life live us.

✦ Fourth, while keeping the heart open and vulnerable, we deeply wish that our loved ones be made free from suffering. We can sustain this wish through silent prayer or by repeating over and over again to ourselves a heartfelt phrase. I use these beautiful words from the ancient meditation on lovingkindness. (The full text is in Appendix 2.)

May all beings be happy;
May they be joyous and live in safety.

Although four steps are described, opening a sacred space is really one single movement out of small-minded thinking into a transpersonal state of mind that includes us, our loved ones, and everything. Extraordinary meetings take place on this common ground of inner healing. The coming together may be silent, or it may take shape in words. The most powerful verbal exchanges are often simple. In the right circumstances, a very short dialogue can produce a flash of mutual understanding. Afterward there may be a longer conversation.

RECEIVING SPIRITUAL CARE

The dying live very close to truth, and their insights can help us. When we listen with careful respect, they will guide and even take care of us. I've seen dying people who gave a great deal of emotional and spiritual support to their friends and loved ones right up to the very last days.

And then there are those who transform into something like a shaman or a guru. Michael, a patient with AIDS, so purified himself through pain and acceptance that his frail body conveyed a compelling love of enormous power. All those gathered around his bed simply glowed. When this happens, the patient becomes a conduit for healing, blessing everyone with a deep sense of well-being. But every death is extraordinary, and every dying person who shares the experience with others gives a great gift.

I enjoy telling people in hospice how much it means to me to be a part of the last days of their lives. My better qualities seem to rise up to match the strenuous effort they are making. I can't help but want to honor their death with the way I live my life. Feeling so much gratitude toward the dying, I resist all notions that spiritual care is anything other than mutual.

DEATH DOESN'T HAVE TO BE "GOOD"

As alternative ways of dying move closer to the mainstream, we hear more talk about the "good death." Dying at home is preferable when possible, but the term *good death* goes beyond choosing the optimal conditions for dying and suggests a preferred style and content.

Good death suggests there is an absolute standard by which to measure whether a death has succeeded or failed. In our ambitious society, where every new trend is marketed and made a status symbol, there is great danger in defining what death ought to look like. Will there come a time when Americans pursue the good death in the same restless way they pursue the good life? Will the proper deathstyle become essential to the proper lifestyle?

Indeed, all of us want to die well. What actually happens is bounded by the way we lived and by circumstance. At the end what we need is not judgment but acceptance of how it worked out for us.

The desire to help a loved one die well springs from the best of intentions, but dying has nothing to do with good or bad or with success or failure. Dying for each of us is life as it is. When we, as caregivers, share with our loved ones a moment of their dying as it actually is—full of pain and confusion and love and joy and fear and awe—we are blessed with a perfect sense of self-sufficiency.

Within the death and dying movement the good death is defined in different ways. Each definition both illumines and obscures what is really going on for the dying person.

Death with dignity is emblazoned on the banner of those protesting unwanted medical interventions that prolong human life long after consciousness has left. This protest deserves our support. The SUPPORT study reported that physicians routinely order the most extreme mechanical measures to keep patients breathing even against their wishes. This ghoulish practice must be stopped.

Unfortunately the death with dignity slogan carries the subtext that death should appear elegant, or at least well behaved, and certainly not ugly. Anyone who reads *How We Die*, the clinically frank best-seller by Sherwin B. Nuland, M.D., knows this expectation is unreal. The physical processes of dying can devastate a person's appearance. But neither death nor dignity has anything to do with the world of appearances. Even if terminal illness makes our bodies look disgusting, as cancer and AIDS so often do, we are inherently dignified because dignity is our human birthright. As caregivers we acknowledge the dignity of our patients by accepting their minds and bodies as they are.

Empowerment, a term taken from political action, is used in the death and dying movement to describe ways to give dying people greater control over their last days. A more enlightened use of narcotics, for example, has empowered hospice patients by liberating them from the grip of pain. Honest communication about death has empowered patients and families to get what they need from medical personnel.

These are important achievements, but putting death and dying in the context of power and politics can distort what's really going on. Yes, dying is a practical process, and we can learn how to cope with its many trying symptoms, but ultimately death demands that we give up control and cultivate the deepest possible acceptance. Death is letting go, and it is this letting go that is liberating.

Peaceful death is the ideal extolled by most religions. Christians hope to "rest in peace"; Jews try to make the last of life as anxiety-free as possible; and Tibetan Buddhists seek a tranquil exit out of this life to enter the next one properly. (Modern medicine responds to the aspiration for peace by providing narcotics; euthanasia is drug pacification taken to an extreme.) As we care for dying loved ones, we can hope they will achieve a peaceful healing of their lives, but we can't make it happen. Despite our best efforts, they may die with muddled minds and in pain. The only thing we can promise is that we will stay with them to the end.

Conscious dying is the catchphrase of those who believe we can ennoble our death by meeting it with a clear mind. At one time the hospice movement endorsed this idea. It was thought people could die both pain-free and mentally clear. Practice showed that even under the best conditions it didn't happen that often. Both pain and the medication used to control it tend to dull consciousness, and some people require deep sedation for extreme pain. Others lapse into delirium or coma as a result of disease.

Although the term *conscious dying* has since fallen out of use among professionals, it still circulates in the death and dying movement. A better term would be *conscious caregiving*.

As conscious caregivers we ask nothing special of our dying loved ones. Consciousness can only be brought to life in ourselves; it can never be pushed on another. If someone wants to deny his death, this is who he is, and we should honor his right to be himself. Simple acceptance is the most profound spiritual care.

Death as growth is the concept introduced in the mid-1970s, when the Swiss psychiatrist Elisabeth Kübler-Ross coauthored a breakthrough book titled *Death: The Final Stage of Growth*. It put dying in the context of that decade's human potential movement by suggesting that death was the culmination of lifelong human development. This insight expanded our sense of the possible, but it is not an evolutionary law. Caregivers should not push their patients toward growth. In fact the highest stage of growth is enlightenment, and it can come to anyone, at any time.

What is enlightenment? It has been described as "feeling like one come back from the dead." This sounds very much like a near-death experience, in which a person judged clinically dead returns to life, having been transformed by the experience. Survival no longer seems like such a struggle, or even very important. The ceaseless striving for a better life in the future falls away, and what is now is enough.

If this kind of spiritual understanding can come through a near-death experience, then death is not a stage of growth but rather a window on what life is. The nature of life is unceasing change. Perceiving that all is change produces an exhilarating sense of freedom. Since we can't hold on to anything, there is nothing to hold on to—so let's have fun!

Near-death survivors really do seem to find new enjoyment in life. Looking through the window of death, they discern what is truly important: to live life fully, deeply, meaningfully—for as long as it lasts.

Three

Meditation Takes Care of Us

Study to be quiet.
—St. Paul

TAKING CARE OF THE DYING is intense work. When we choose to be caregivers, we put ourselves in the presence of our loved ones' pain and suffering. We can't change these circumstances, but we can change the way we respond to them by relaxing the mind through meditation.

Dozens of books laud the way meditation lowers blood pressure, calms the nerves, strengthens self-esteem, lifts depression, reduces cholesterol, sharpens concentration, and raises awareness. It sounds too good to be true. A friend of mine attended a workshop given by Gary Snyder, the Pulitzer Prize–winning poet who studied meditation in Japan. Afterward my friend sent me a skeptical letter. "OK," he wrote, "so meditation can make you love your dog and your job, but how?"

Meditation lightens the mind. As we sit, motionless except for our breathing, heavy thoughts and feelings float off like clouds. Some are white and fluffy, others dark and threatening; we don't much care. Letting the clouds pass, we focus instead on the big sky behind. Boundaries blur and dissolve, and we feel quiet and steady inside.

Meditation gives us rest, and when we are rested, we are better caregivers. Under Medicare, a patient can be readmitted to a hospital for five days to give respite to the home caregiver. Meditation is respite available every day.

Meditation reduces stress and improves effectiveness, but it is more than a self-improvement technique. Meditation is a deeply liberating spiritual practice. The power comes from its strong similarity to death. Meditation and dying are two different names for the same thing—letting go.

There is a monkey trap made from a hollowed-out coconut with bait inside. The monkey reaches in, but the hole in the coconut is so small the monkey can't extract its paw while gripping the bait. Of course the monkey could loosen its fist and escape. Instead it clings and gets caught, not by the hunter but by its own unwillingness to let go.

Death forces us to let go of our bodies and move on; meditation teaches us to let go willingly. The tight fist slowly opens. We stop resisting change and find certainty in the flow of life as it is.

TWO KINDS OF MEDITATION

The ways to meditate are many, but they fall into two broad categories: those that do *something* and those that do *nothing*.

Do-something meditation tightens concentration. To control the rambling mind the meditator narrows the field of attention to one thing only. This can be done by reciting a mantra or visualizing a sacred image or making a belly-based sound, such as in the "aahh breath" described in the Home Skill section at the end of Chapter 8. The resulting trancelike mental state can be soothing and very pleasurable.

Do-nothing meditation broadens concentration. It cultivates an inclusive, rather than exclusive, awareness. The mind is lifted to the intense and broad wakefulness sometimes seen in wild animals. Like a swinging door, the mind is kept open to allow everything occurring to pass through. Sounds, movements, and light shifts originating "outside" as well as thoughts and feelings from "inside" enter and exit unhindered.

Do-something meditation quiets the mind through the power of positive thinking. Do-nothing meditation frees the mind by accepting its contents and then letting them go. And acceptance is the greatest power of all.

HOW TO PRACTICE DO-NOTHING MEDITATION

This form of meditation is made up of two components, breath and posture. A stable posture provides the physical structure for containing the mind and allowing it to settle. The settled mind is kept awake and alert by counting each breath. The posture becomes the center of the physical world, and the breath becomes the center of the mental world.

First, the breath.

The person new to meditation can develop an appreciation of breathing by simply lying comfortably on the floor in a quiet place. Even experienced meditators find this position helpful when they are tired.

1. Lying on your back, take three deep breaths and then settle into your normal breathing pattern, breathing comfortably from a soft, relaxed belly.

2. Lie motionless. Silently count your breaths one after the other. Start over when you reach ten, or whenever you lose count. Continue counting your breaths for as long as you meditate.

3. As you breathe, observe the rhythm of your breath with an attitude of discovery. Notice the length of the inhale and exhale, and then let your focus glide to the exhalation. Imagine that it is lengthening and deepening. Don't try to force anything; judgment just gets in the way. Note what's happening without asking why. Just let it happen naturally, and breathe, counting one . . . two . . . three. . . .

Now, the posture.

Applying effort to maintain an erect sitting posture will put energy into your meditation, making you alert and refreshed.

1. Place a straight-backed wooden chair facing a wall so you won't be distracted. Sit down solidly in the chair, putting both feet flat on the floor and a few inches apart. You might want to put a thin cushion between your back and the back of the chair. If your feet don't reach the floor, rest them on a cushion.

2. Loosen your belt, let your stomach hang out naturally, and straighten your spine by pushing up gently from the buttocks. Feel the push all the way to the back of the head. Your bottom should be the foundation for your entire back, shoulders, and head. Don't lift from the shoulders; release the shoulders completely and push up from your "sitting bones," the bony protuberances you feel against the seat of the chair.

3. Your head should be up, chin slightly in, and ears in line with the shoulders. Keep your eyes cast down, and let the lids droop without shutting the eyes. Closing your eyes can make you dreamy, but if you really need to, go ahead.

4. Put your hands in your lap in the meditation position, with one hand resting in the palm of the other, take three deep breaths, then slide easily into breath counting.

The essential task in do-nothing meditation is *not* to try to accomplish anything in particular. Just stay attentive to what's going on, and accept it. Through the process of bringing the mind back again and again to the breath—realizing that we are not fully "here," and then returning again to being here—we stumble on an amazing discovery. We don't have to be anything special; we only have to be.

JUST DO IT

There are many variations on the basic model, but meditation isn't something to talk about too much. Just do it, if only for a short time. Ten minutes a day or even every other day is plenty in the beginning. The idea is to build a habit that works for you. The practice tends to build on itself if you can keep a regular schedule. Compare the way you feel when you meditate with the way you feel when you don't, and you're likely to want to continue.

Sitting with others can amplify the impact; you might suggest this to your caregiver support group as a good way to open meetings. Sit quietly together and enjoy the relaxation and uplifting intimacy of silence.

Don't be afraid to include in your meditation meaningful practices of your own religious or spiritual tradition. Some caregivers like to mix in a few minutes of prayer or visualization or the silent repetition of a meaningful phrase. Then they return again to simple breath counting. Any method is fine as long as it is done with awareness. Meditation is not an ideology. Just do it.

Any time is fine for meditation except after meals. A full stomach can make you drowsy, and keeping track of the breath is hard enough as it is. Sometimes even counting higher than "one" can feel like a real accomplishment, but that's OK. We sit in silence without judgment.

Sitting motionless, observing our needy, expectant thoughts, we patiently set them aside again and again and return to our breath. It's more grunt work than mysticism, but if we can stick to it, there is ample testimony that over the weeks and months and years, meditation brings serenity and greater self-understanding.

A cautionary note: Although meditation is a wonderful practice for a caregiver, it is not something to push on a dying person who has never meditated and has no strong interest in starting. In the early stages of actively dying, right after the doctor's prognosis is received, meditation can help calm the mind to accomplish needed tasks. Later the dissolution of body and mind that dying involves may frustrate the focused mental discipline of meditation. Dying is hard work; there's no need to make it more difficult.

CAREGIVING AND MEDITATION

"Meditation may take one out of the world," says Gary Snyder, "but it also puts one totally into it."[1] Caregiving is exactly this mixture of mundane and transcendental. In one moment you might be searching for your patient's missing sock; in the next it's your patient's life that is missing!

Meditation and caregiving are mutually supportive. Developing awareness of breath and posture trains us to pay attention to our patients. And the expansive mind that meditation makes possible frees us to take the appropriate action even though it might challenge convention-bound notions of what is right.

Above all, meditation makes us sensitive to both the details and the big picture. We pay attention to what is going on inside *and* outside. We are fully conscious caregivers.

By the same token, caring for the dying is on-the-job training in meditation. The patient's pace in speech and activity can be excruciatingly slow, and dying may seem to drag on cruelly. This slow unwinding can give rise to impatience. Some books advise caregivers to find distraction by making calls, doing crafts, balancing a checkbook, or performing other routine tasks while sitting with the patient. Escape is sometimes necessary, but for spiritual growth you don't want to keep your mind off your work; you want to put your mind *into* your work in the focused way that meditation encourages.

Meditation cultivates the wisdom that comes from studying our actions. We sit, we wait, and we watch. With an alert inner eye, we note what we do and feel at the bedside. When does intuition guide us to do the right thing? And when do we find ourselves pushing too hard to make something happen just to satisfy our own needs?

"The challenge of hospice work," says Paul Haller, "is to notice. I think it's too much to say, 'Just be infinite kindness and generosity.' I think it's more realistic to say, 'Try to notice our needs.'" With a meditative mind we can watch and accept our needs, and not be controlled by them.

In the work of acceptance, the belly is a helpful guide. When a painful situation arises at the bedside, the belly tends to stiffen in resistance. This is tiring. Constantly monitor the belly to keep it supple. When tension is felt, identify the cause. Then take a breath and soften the belly into acceptance. Keeping a soft belly softens pain and helps to dissipate it.

The most painful feelings are those that touch our fear of death. We must acknowledge and befriend these feelings to be of service to the loved ones in our care. To get closer to a dying person we have to get closer to our own fear of death. Meditation helps us do it.

MEDITATION AND DEATH

In periods of meditation we let go of each doubt and fear and pain as it arises. In this way we travel the same passage as our patients. Dying is the most profound letting go, and, like being born, it takes persistent effort. By matching our effort in meditation with our loved ones' effort in dying, we share their acute experience of mortality.

This is how the dying encourage us to appreciate our own lives more. We show our gratitude by caring for them with the unselfish awareness of big, meditative mind.

When our meditation is deep, when we really let go, we perceive that what we call our life actually belongs to the universe. The storms of confusion clear, revealing the place of pure potentiality. In these moments, "you are not seeing or thinking," says Suzuki-roshi, "you are actually one with everything."[2]

Becoming one with everything does not mean becoming nothing at all. Through meditation we find peace—not in the permanence of our particular life, since that is impossible, but in the continuity of all life. In the words of Basho,

Within your life and mine
there lives
a cherry blossom.[3]

II

Caregiver's Mind

When you give something you feel good, because at that
time you feel at one with what you are giving.
— Shunryu Suzuki-roshi

Four

The Craft of Patient Care

The more we understand particular things,
the more we understand God.
                                    —Spinoza

T HIS CHAPTER BEGINS the section on direct patient care, the practical heart of this book. We come to caregiving because we
want to get closer to the profound experience of dying, but dying
is a necessary and completely natural event. We deepen our relationship to it in very pragmatic and ordinary ways.

Caregiving nurtures our spirits with everydayness. We don't need
to withdraw from the surface of things to find deeper meaning. Direct patient care—the physical work of feeding, cleaning, moving,
and maintaining our loved ones in bed—makes their dying a lived
reality for us.

The loving power of that reality runs through the following excerpt, taken from the notebooks of Louis Vega, a veteran volunteer.

> So I turn on Monte's space heater and I get the warm soapy
> water and towels. I let him choose his clean clothes. Then I
> put on the latex gloves and I help him out of his wet shirt. Of
> course we get his hands and arms and head tangled up in his
> shirt, a little comedy.
>
> We decide that a "bed bath" with Monte sitting on a chair is
> easiest, so he gets out of bed and onto the chair and I wash his
> upper body. He still has some meat on him; he hasn't started

wasting yet. I help him into a clean T-shirt and cover his back with his robe. Then off come his wet pants, diaper, and socks. I wash the rest of his body as quickly as possible because he is complaining of the cold. The temperature of the water is fine, he says, but he's still cold. I comfort him as best as I can.

"You're cold because the water is evaporating off your body," I explain. "So, you feel cool, like when you go swimming on a hot day."

"Oh," he says.

I dry him as quickly as possible. Now he is clean and dry and wearing fresh clothes.

"OK?" I ask him.

"OK," he says. "But I hope this is the last diaper change for today!"

"I hope so too," I say. "For your sake."

Caregiving is love, but it's a love that's tempered through action. A person lying on a wet bed needs a change of sheets before she can be cuddled. Relieving discomfort is our primary job, and the work can be difficult. Attending to the shifting needs and symptoms of a dying person demands stamina and attention to detail. Doing the work well, with no expectations, we find satisfaction in *craft*.

Any techniques we may need to know—how to handle an oxygen tank, put on a condom catheter, give an injection, respond to a seizure—can be easily taught by the visiting hospice nurse. Far more important is the natural wisdom that arises from listening closely to our loved ones and responding from the heart.

Caregiving is a tender craft we learn by doing. When we do it with awareness, it will change our lives. Patient care is so constant and so challenging that it can alter the old, stale ways we see ourselves. Insight arises from the work's contradictions. We are engaged in feeding our loved ones and keeping them clean, dry, and alive, but they are engaged in dying. No matter what we do to improve the quality of their lives, they will have to give life up.

Accepting this paradox, letting go of our goals for improving either their lives or ours, we are free to celebrate existence just as it is. Grateful for the opportunity to share love with our patients, we adapt to the ebb and flow of their napping, chatting, eating, bathing, and defecating. We find our place in the fluid, shape-shifting, eternal moment of the present.

SETTING UP THE BEDROOM

The dying person's bed is the center of his life; locate the bed in a place that is both practical for caregivers and pleasing to the patient. A first-floor room close to the hub of household activity saves stair climbing and lets the patient feel a part of what's going on. A room with a view is best; what a patient sees from her window can be vital to her.

Since a dying person's world is usually not much more than one room, try to bring as much beauty as possible into it, but remember that beauty is in the eye of the beholder. That ugly old baseball pennant may carry some lovely memories. Arrange the furniture in a way that allows your loved one to feed and take care of himself as much as possible. Making the effort to eat, brush the teeth, bathe, and get to the toilet promotes a sense of self-worth, counters depression, and stimulates mental clarity.

Place the bed away from the walls to make sheet changing easier. The mattress should be rigid enough to prevent sagging but soft enough to conform to the natural curves of the body. Protect the mattress with a plastic sheet or mattress cover. A bed board of quarter-inch plywood cut to the size of the mattress adds extra support. An **egg-crate mattress** laid bumpy side up on top of the regular mattress eases pressure on tender skin and reduces the risk of bedsores.

A motorized **hospital bed** obtained from a rental company is usually best. Hospital beds have electric or manual controls to adjust the height of the mattress. This permits patient care to be performed with minimal strain on both caregiver and patient. The hospital bed mattress can be raised when giving a bed bath or a massage, and it can be lowered to allow the patient to get into and out of bed more easily. The mattress can also be elevated at the head to bring the patient into a sitting position and at the knees to relieve swollen ankles and feet. Hospital beds have pull-up side rails that prevent people from falling out of bed and restrain those who become confused or restless and want to wander. And the beds can be easily adapted for an overhead, triangle-shaped **trapeze** that gives weakened patients more independence by letting them pull themselves up to a sitting position.

Hospital beds can be helpful to both caregiver and patient, but some people don't want to give up their familiar beds for a piece of shiny chrome hardware. If your patient prefers her own bed, its mattress should be elevated to about the height of the primary caregiver's hips to facilitate patient care procedures. In this case a **foam wedge** and pillows can be used to raise the head or feet. If your loved one becomes very fragile over time, and getting her into and out of bed is hazardous, you may have to insist gently on bringing in an adjustable hospital bed.

ALL ABOUT EQUIPMENT

Other kinds of equipment and various modifications to the household can increase the dying person's sense of independence and safety. A bedside **commode** is essential. Put one in the room when you set it up even if the commode isn't yet needed. Fear of not being able to get to the bathroom in time can lead to constipation. A screen by the bed will let the patient use the commode with some degree of dignity. A **cane,** a **walker,** or a **wheelchair**—

sometimes all three—may be needed for mobility. Wheelchairs are not all the same. Have a look at what the rental company offers. Wheelchairs with sharp right-angle seats can be a problem for those who have trouble sitting upright.

Wheelchairs don't always fit the compressed living spaces of city dwellers. A **rolling chair** can be improvised from an armless kitchen or dining room chair with wheels or casters attached to the legs. The rolling chair has two advantages: it can turn on its axis, and it is narrow enough to pass through a bathroom door. The disadvantage is that it has no brake and must be steadied when the patient is getting in or out.

A **grab bar** and a **raised toilet seat** can aid in standing up after using the toilet. **Rails** and a bath chair in the tub or shower will increase bathing safety and comfort. Nonskid **bath mats** are a must.

Set up the space by the bed with care. The bedside nightstand can become so cluttered with medicines, lotions, and toilet necessities that there's little room for items of personal pleasure, such as a radio, books, tapes, framed photographs, and letters. Keep a calendar and a clock with a lighted face in the room to orient your loved one to date and time. Physical care items should be kept on a separate **caregiving cart** that can be pulled to the bed as necessary. A wheeled kitchen vegetable bin will work if it has a level surface on top to hold a basin for bed baths.

Put a comfortable chair by the bed for visitors and to hold the patient's bathrobe. **Hospital-style gowns** that open in back are easiest to get on and off when someone has trouble sitting up, but in the early stages he may not want this much rearward exposure! Don't introduce specialized clothes or equipment prematurely. A cane doesn't represent freedom of mobility to a person who would rather walk unaided.

I have mixed feelings about television. It can be a source of stimulation and a very effective distraction from pain. But it can also numb consciousness as potently as any narcotic, and the sound can irritate others in the household. Try to help your loved one use this tool wisely. I do like videocassette recorders, however. Watching a video together can be a pleasant kind of sharing. If the TV and VCR are kept on a wheeled cart, they can be moved into the room for favorite shows and then taken out again to encourage other activities.

A **space heater** and a **fan** will offset fluctuations in the dying person's body temperature. The fan is also useful for dispelling toilet odors and making the room more inviting for visitors. Don't forget the **hot-water bottle.** It is both an excellent pain reliever and a great source of comfort.

In the kitchen, a **blender** is essential for preparing purees (the all-important "smoothies") and for mixing food supplements into soups and drinks. Also helpful are a juicer, a microwave, a toaster oven, and an ice crusher. A food processor does a quick job of cutting up vegetables for nonchew recipes.

GETTING COMFORTABLE

Make the bed an environment that conveys a sense of comfort but can be easily cleaned and maintained. When the person is continent for most of the time, a rubberized flannel **undersheet** can be laid on top of the plastic mattress cover to soften and warm it. If incontinence develops, the undersheet can be moved up one layer and laid on top of the regular bottom sheet to help keep it clean and dry. A **Chux underpad,** placed with the plastic side down, or **adult diapers** that have been spread open, are alternate ways to protect the bottom sheet.

In cold weather flannel sheets and pillowcases provide warmth and pleasure. Another source of warm comfort is the fluffy synthetic **sheepskin** available from hospital suppliers. This yard-square washable pad is placed under the person while she lies in bed or sits in a chair to relieve pressure and prevent bedsores. **Sheepskin-lined booties** can be used to protect the pressure-sensitive heels of those who are bedridden. Build a "tent" for sore feet by placing pillows at the corners of the foot of the bed and then pulling the blankets over the pillows.

Changing and washing sheets is an ongoing activity. It can be a lot of work for both for you and your patient, especially if he is completely bedridden. The Home Skill section at the end of the chapter explains how to change sheets with someone still in the bed.

You'll need to change the sheets whenever they are dirty or wet or whenever your loved one just wants to freshen up. Sheets may last for two or three days, or you may have to change them several times in a single day during bouts of incontinence.

To help keep sheets free from occasional drips, spills, and spit-ups, put a stack of hand towels close by for use as tablecloths, bibs, and handkerchiefs. Soiled sheets, towels, and clothing should be machine-washed as promptly as possible in hot (160°F) soapy water to prevent transmission of infection.

PREVENTING BEDSORES

The weight of the body constantly pushing down on the shoulders, elbows, hips, tailbone, ankles, heels, and buttocks can cause breaks in the skin that become ulcerated and are prone to infection. A bedridden person needs to change position every two to three hours to avoid painful bedsores. (See the following section, "Moving Someone in Bed.")

Bedsores are a serious problem, and dying people are especially susceptible to them. Loss of appetite and the disease process waste away the body mass that cushions bony protuberances. Circulation becomes sluggish, reducing the flow of nutrients, and tissue has little resistance to deterioration. Dampness from incontinence and sweat further irritates the skin.

Prevention is the best treatment.

✦ Try to keep the bottom sheet free from deep wrinkles that can irritate the skin. Do the same with the drawsheet, if one is used (see p.63). Most important, shift the person on a regular schedule from side to side, from back to front, and from lying down to sitting up. You may have to persuade her to cooperate. She may not want to give up a warm and comfortable position, but you really must insist. Explain why it's necessary, and then sit with your loved one afterward for a while to help her adjust.

✦ As you help the patient change position, check his skin on the side that was just facing the bed. Any redness should disappear within five minutes. If it doesn't, change position more often. Red spots that don't fade within a minute should be gently massaged to stimulate circulation and strengthen tissue.

✦ Pillows placed between flexed knees and under the ankles and elbows will relieve pressure on these joints. Latex **doughnuts** can be put under elbows and heels when the patient is on her back, or the calves and forearms can be lifted with small pillows. Lying on a sheepskin or an egg-crate mattress (but not both) relieves pressure on the skin. If the patient is not allergic to it, fabric softener can be added during washing to reduce friction from the sheets. When redness persists, tell the hospice nurse.

✦ Finally, if a bedsore does occur, clean it with soap and water and seek professional advice.

MOVING SOMEONE IN BED

Before you do any bedside procedure, ask the patient's permission if at all possible. We should let those who are losing control of their lives make as many decisions as they can. Explain what you're going to do and why you need to do it. Offer this explanation even if the person is comatose; he may be able to hear you. In any case, speaking to a patient is a way to remind yourself that you're dealing with a person, not a body.

Moving someone in bed carries a risk of back injury. Take your time, and plan your move. Pay attention to body mechanics. Be mindful of the differences in body mass between you and your patient, and use leverage as much as possible. Don't bend from the waist to pick up or lift—bend your knees, stoop down, and lift using your thigh muscles while keeping your back straight and your head up. Hold the person close to your middle, at your center of gravity.

A better alternative to lifting your patient is to position yourself so you can slide, pull, or roll her. When pulling a person in bed toward you, keep your feet apart and put one foot forward so you're not off balance. The hospice nurse can demonstrate these and other ways to avoid strain.

In helping your loved one move, avoid doing what he can do for himself. Overhelping robs the person of much-needed exercise and may undermine his sense of integrity. Encourage your patient to play a part in any procedure by cueing him with a "ready, set, go" signal.

After your loved one can no longer walk or even stand up, she may be able to sit up on her own or by using an overhead trapeze. If she becomes too weak to sit up, she may still be able to pull herself to one side of the bed or the other. Acknowledge these movements as important accomplishments.

People tend to slide down toward the foot of the bed. To help a person move up in bed, have him lie on his back and bend his knees so he's "standing" his bent legs with the feet flat on the sheets. Then, as you stand on the side of the bed, slide your hands and forearms under the patient's back and thighs. With a "ready, set, go," have him scoot himself up by pushing with the heels while you lean your weight sideways toward the head of the bed, pulling your loved one with you.

When the person has become so weak that she must rely entirely on the caregiver to move, it's time to start using the drawsheet. This handy device lets you slide or tug someone up or down in bed and from side to side, using a folded sheet as a toboggan.

The drawsheet is simply a regular sheet that has been doubled over and tucked in perpendicular to the bottom sheet. Locate the drawsheet underneath the person's body from hips to head. The folded edge of the doubled drawsheet should be nearest the head of the bed.

The two ends of the drawsheet are kept tucked under the mattress until it's time for a move. Then, if two caregivers are present, the drawsheet ends are loosened and rolled inward to form parallel "ropes" close to the person's body. These rolled sheet ends serve as handles for the caregivers. Standing one on each side of the bed, the caregivers grasp their rolled drawsheet ends and together shift the person in the desired direction. When there is only one caregiver, the person's arms are folded across the chest. The caregiver then stands at the head of the bed and tugs on the drawsheet to pull the person upward.

To help a weakened person lie on his side, raise the opposite side rail on the hospital bed, if you have one. Have him reach over and grasp the rail, or the far edge of the bed, as best he can. Then, placing yourself on the side of the bed your patient is being turned toward, grasp his far hip with one hand and far shoulder with the other. You are now standing with both arms extended across your loved one's body as he lies on his back. Spread your feet apart and, with one foot slightly behind you, lean back and gently roll the person toward you. Have pillows or a folded blanket handy to tuck behind the back and hips to support him in this position.

GETTING IN AND OUT OF BED

It's important for bedridden people to get up and out of bed as regularly and for as long as their health permits. Unused muscles quickly lose strength. A change of environment provides exercise and freshens morale, and these, in turn, stimulate appetite.

We want to encourage independence and the sense of self-worth that it nourishes, but dying people can be unaware how much illness has weakened them. They may try to walk when they shouldn't.

Be alert to any danger of your patient suffering a damaging fall. Falls are all too common.

You and your loved one will have to experiment to find the ways of getting into and out of bed that work safely for both of you. The best movements and procedures will depend on your relative body sizes, whether or not you have a hospital bed, and the patient's strength.

Here is a standard method for moving someone who is very weak into a chair, wheelchair, or bedside commode without causing injury to either patient or caregiver.

✦ Place the chair, wheelchair (with brakes locked), or commode right alongside you as you stand by the bed, turning the back of the chair toward the foot of the bed. If it's a hospital bed, lower the mattress to make it level with the seat of the chair or commode and drop the side rail. If it's a regular bed, the mattress should be permanently adjusted to the height of the commode in order to make bed-to-toilet transfers easier.

✦ Next, have the patient move close to your edge of the bed and sit up if possible. Then have him swing his legs around and rest his feet on the floor.

If the person can't sit up:

1. Keep up the side rail on the hospital bed and have your loved one use it to pull himself to you. Then drop the rail.

If the patient is too weak to pull himself, you pull him over, getting him to help as much as possible. Do this in stages. First put your hands under the pillow with your palms up and pull over the patient's head and shoulders. Next do the same with the hips, and then with the knees and ankles.

2. Using the method explained in the previous section, roll the patient onto his side, facing you. Raise the head of the hospital bed if you have one. If you are tall, it may also help to elevate the entire bed so you won't have to bend down and hurt your back.

3. Slide your loved one's legs partially over the edge of the bed.

Then reach around and hold him behind the shoulders with one arm, extending the hand upward to hold the neck. With the other hand, gently pull the patient toward you and into an upright position. Continue the movement by using that hand to swing the legs around so the feet are now touching the floor and the person is sitting on the edge of the bed. (If his feet don't reach the floor, you can lower the hospital bed.)

✦ The person is now sitting on the bed facing you. At this point, pause so you can both catch your breath and get balanced. Then reach under the patient's armpits and hold his back at the shoulder blades. If the pressure of your hands causes pain, you might clasp your hands together and hug the patient to you.

✦ Finally, lean back with your butt extended for maximum leverage and raise the person slightly from the edge of the bed. Pivot around a quarter turn toward the chair or wheelchair and lower him onto it. Whew!

With practice you can do this movement using a lot of leverage and very little strength, but if the person is heavy, you may need a helper. Please be careful and don't hurt yourself.

BATHING AND CLEANING

A person confined to bed needs daily bathing for proper hygiene and to maintain a sense of well-being. How much effort this requires depends on the patient's condition. Some people are able to get out of bed and walk or roll to the bathroom up until a few days before they die. Others need to be bathed in their room or their bed for many weeks.

Whatever the work, it's well worth it. The regular ritual of bathing gives shape to an otherwise formless day. Bath time is a good time for a change of sheets, clean clothes, and a fresh point of view. Bathing eliminates odors that can discourage visitors. It stimulates sluggish circulation and provides exercise for a person who gets little of it. And for those who can get to a tub, splashing around in warm water is relaxing and fun. Keep **bubble bath** handy.

A space heater in the bathroom will create a nice cozy environment, but be cautious about burns and electric shocks. Use a mild soap, preferably one that contains cold cream. Soaps with perfumes dry the skin. If your loved one takes tub baths, fill the tub with water that is the temperature she likes. When helping someone into or out of a tub or shower, observe the basics of good body mechanics. This moment is fraught with accident potential. Be extremely careful about slippery bathroom floors. Make sure there are soft, dry towels and a change of clothes handy. Offer to scrub the patient's back or shampoo her hair.

Give your loved one plenty of time in the bathroom, but don't go very far away and be alert to any requests for help. Bathing can make an ill person very tired; keep a chair handy. She may prefer to sit in it and wash from the sink.

When the person can no longer get up, bathing is done from a basin placed next to the bed. Use a washcloth, two towels, and soap in a dish. The water should feel warm to the inside of your wrist. Change the water several times during the bath. Make sure the room is warm and there's a towel or blanket available to cover up during the bath. Give the person all the privacy she wants.

Your patient should do as much bathing as possible, even if this is only washing face and hands. The caregiver does what the patient can't. Bathe from the top down, cleaning the face, chest and stomach, arms and hands, and finally the groin, legs, and feet. Clean the genital area gently and well; odors collect here. Rinse off the soap, blot the skin dry, and apply a lanolin-based lotion.

HAIR CARE

Our hair is a big part of who we are. Keeping it washed and combed or brushed feels good and looks good. Try to wash the person's hair whenever he asks, or at least once a week. Shampooing can be done in bed by having the patient lie on his back with his head over the edge of the bed. You then support the head with one hand and wash the hair with the other, using a basin of warm water. A bucket catches the drips. Rinse by pouring clean water over the hair and into the bucket. If your loved one is easily tired, check with a hospital supply company for "no rinse" shampoos that can be sprayed or combed directly into the hair.

Before giving a shampoo, you might offer to massage the scalp, and also the head, neck, face, and shoulders. This is easy to perform, and patients usually find it a relaxing and comforting experience.

Men's hair doesn't normally require more than washing and combing, but women enjoy having their hair styled. The hospice nurse should know beauticians who are trained in hospital care. Having your loved one's hair done professionally makes a nice present for a special occasion.

PILLS, PILLS, PILLS

Dying people must take lots of medication to relieve their many distressing symptoms. Caregivers who are suspicious of pills will soon discover how important they can be for a dying person's quality of life.

The caregiver is responsible for seeing that pills and other medicines are taken correctly. Here are some tips:

✦ Give the medication as soon as possible after it's been opened or crushed.

✦ Before offering medication with food or liquid, make sure the two are compatible.

✦ When crushing a tablet, put it in a plastic bag and mash it with a blunt object.

✦ Have the person sit up to take medication.

✦ Before giving medication in powder form lubricate the mouth and throat with a sip of liquid and let the patient rinse afterward.

✦ Avoid waking the person at night to take medications. Insomnia can be a problem for bedridden patients.

✦ Here are some medical notations for prescriptions: QD means the medication is taken daily, BID is twice daily, TID is three times daily, and PO means taken by mouth. PRN means taken whenever the patient requests; you'll see this one often.

In hospice, most medications are administered orally, but there's no reason for the home caregiver to shy away from giving injections if necessary. It's really a simple process. The visiting nurse can show you how.

Keeping track of many medications can be tricky. The **Mediset** is a big help. This is a clear plastic "med box" available at drugstores. It contains separate compartments for each set of pills to be taken at prescribed times in the day. The patient's weekly pill schedule can be taped to the back of the box. Each time medications are given, make an entry in the Patient Log (see the Home Skill section at the end of Chapter 7). Also record the patient's responses to the medication.

Many home hospice services offer a symptom relief kit containing emergency medications for use when medical personnel aren't readily available. Check with your hospice nurse about this.

INSOMNIA

Giving your patient, and yourself, a good night's sleep can be a challenge. Patient sleeplessness is probably the single greatest cause of caregiver burnout. Anxiety, lack of exercise, depression, fear of nighttime incontinence, loneliness, pain and restlessness, night sweats, and nightmares can keep a dying person tossing and turning. Many patients simply do not distinguish between night and day. They doze off and then wake up in the middle of the night wanting company.

Medications are available to aid sleep, but try other means first. Stimulating activities will encourage your patient to stay awake during the day so she can sleep at night. Massage, soft music, guided imagery audiotapes, and alcoholic drinks such as hot brandy are all ways to induce sleep.

During periods of patient insomnia, the chore of staying up all night should be shared among caregivers.

Home Skill: Making a Bed with Someone in It

The bed is the center of a dying person's world. Keeping the bed clean, dry, and comfortable is a big part of the caregiver's job. When the person doesn't have the strength to get out of bed, the sheets are changed while she is still in it. If she loses control of bladder or bowels, this may be necessary several times a day.

This work is very physical; don't let it exhaust you. Use good body mechanics. Pause to soften your belly with a deep breath when you feel anxious or tired. Use a helper if one is available. Calm your mind and watch your movements. Make each bed change interesting by approaching it with a sense of wanting to improve your craft.

Always begin by explaining what you plan to do and asking permission to do it. Keep the patient warm and comforted while wet sheets are being stripped or painful limbs are being moved. It may be pleasant to put on some music or play the radio, but intimate silence is also nice.

The basic strategy is to strip and change one-half of the bed at a time. Here's the twelve-step program!

1. Assemble clean linens. Have an extra blanket or a robe handy for keeping the person warm.

2. Raise the hospital bed mattress to a comfortable height for you to work. Drop the side rails.

3. Loosen the bedding on all sides. Remove any unneeded pillows.

4. Take off the bedspread, blankets, and top sheet, and cover the person with the extra blanket or the robe.

5. Have the person turn toward the opposite side of the bed, or roll her on her side.

6. Facing the patient's back, gather the soiled bottom sheet lengthwise in a flat roll and push it close to her. Do the same with the drawsheet, if one is used. Smooth the mattress pad.

7. Lay out the clean sheet along your side of the bed, leaving about eighteen inches at the head so it can be tucked in securely. Push the length of clean sheet toward the back of the person's body. If the soiled sheet is dry, the clean one should be pushed under it. Otherwise keep the two sheets close but separated.

8. Tuck in the clean sheet at the head and along the side. Lay the person's feet on the clean sheet by lifting them from under the ankles.

9. If a drawsheet is used, lay out a fresh one along the clean side of the bed and tuck it in under the mattress. Push the clean drawsheet against the person's body and under the soiled sheet, or close to it if the soiled sheet is wet.

10. On signal, help the person roll back over the hump of bunched soiled and clean sheets so she ends up facing you. Cover and keep her warm.

11. Move to the other side of the bed and pull away the dirty sheet. Smooth the mattress pad and tuck in the clean bottom sheet and the drawsheet.

12. Help the person get centered in the middle of the bed and cover her with a top sheet.

Five

Acceptance Is Everything

I remember someone complaining to
me, "All I do is take people out to smoke
cigarettes. And I hate smoking, and I don't
think it's good for them."

What could I say? A box of matches is a
very useful item for a volunteer to have.

—Paul Haller

DEATH IS SO MYSTERIOUS that we must approach it without expectations. Not only the hour of our death but also its content
and quality are unknown. Some dying people grow and change in
the process, and some don't seem to.

As caregivers we nurture whatever growth is possible by empty-
ing our minds of preconceptions. We simply devote our full attention to our patients and give them what they need most—total
acceptance. Acceptance is the caregiver's most valuable gift to the
patient.

This gift is not so easy to deliver. Our personal agendas get in the
way. We find ourselves striving to do good when all patients want
is for us to be there with them while they go through their changes.

Among those I saw change intensely was John Gunter. This account of his dying is taken from my journals.

John arrived at hospice not long after retiring from a well-
paid union job and opening a small shop with Nancy, his lovely

young wife. They shared an eleven-year-old daughter, lots of friends and nearby relatives, and a bright future. Then John learned he had liver cancer and only a few months to live.

Despite his wasted physical condition, he remained a handsome man with a thick, black mustache and a ready smile who made friends easily. I felt a connection. We were fathers, native San Franciscans, and exactly the same age. As I took him around the hospital grounds in his wheelchair, the hope arose that something special might develop between us. Perhaps I could teach him things I'd learned from my hospice work; perhaps I could help him die more easily.

John had a totally different agenda: he didn't want to die at all. Although now painfully thin, he had been a serious athlete, and as we sat in the garden he would pump away at a hand exerciser with all his flagging energy. He was determined to "get back in shape" and "get out of here," he said.

One day he told me he needed a portable wheelchair ramp so he could get his chair into his van and could go home for the weekends. I offered to phone the rental agencies, and this pleased him, but on the way back to the ward his mood shifted. Suddenly I could do nothing right. With every bump in the path he gave me a contemptuous glare. Did I have to push him so fast? How long had I been doing this, anyway? And on and on. I finished my shift not at all sure I could ever get close to him.

I made some calls about the ramp and then called the hospice. John wasn't going anywhere, I was told. He had become very irritable; his wife had confided to staff that she didn't think she could manage having him at home.

The next time I came I found him sleeping with eyes open, evidence of atrophied eye muscles. He was getting worse, and he knew it. Of course the only way he would get "better" was to complete the dying process, but I couldn't tell him that. Still, we always found a lot to talk about. John liked to keep a conversation going as a way to ward off the cold. Silence was threatening. Whenever I lapsed into it he would get angry. "What are you doing—meditating?" he bellowed at me one day. Actually, I was, but this wasn't what he wanted from me. To him my silence was a meddlesome intrusion. I left that day convinced I wouldn't be teaching John anything. It didn't feel good. Obviously my expectations had set me up for a fall.

Then his fear began to take him over. In the course of the next week he had a panic attack masquerading as bouts of severe shortness of breath. Oxygen helped, but the fear was uncontrollable, and the doctor prescribed antipsychotic drugs to contain it. I would have preferred meditation to medication, but John's situation was too urgent. "There's no peace inside John Gunter," the doctor said. "He might be one of the rare ones who die with difficulty." These were ominous words.

A few more weeks passed, and then the end came. In early November I arrived to find John moved to the "quiet room." He lay on his back motionless, keeping his eyes closed even when awake. I thought perhaps his fear was so great he saw enemies everywhere so he chose not to see anyone at all. When I entered and quietly greeted him, my words only made him clench up. I started to leave but he whispered, "Don't go."

For more than an hour I stood motionless by his bed, my mind empty of everything except his breath and mine. The work was one extending support from a distance. I kept myself in contact with him, but I didn't try to push it too far. What this "contact" was I can't explain, but it was real. When I left, I knew we'd said good-bye.

On the following Tuesday, Eileen, the volunteer coordinator, called and left a message. John had died at 5:40 P.M. The family came, and they filled the room, she said. "They were just where they needed to be, so it was quite lovely. Now John is out. I don't know how resolved he was at the end; I can only hope that something became clear, but he was a great guy. I think we did well by him here just by accepting him."

The other shoe fell when Paul Kelley, the hospice social worker, related his eyewitness account. Over the years Paul has known hundreds of dying people, but he said John's death was particularly beautiful. "There was such stillness and peace," he said. "The air was thick with it."

"SUFFERING WITH"

Supported by family and friends and contained by medication, John went through many twists and turns in his dying. Did he achieve what he had to do? Who can say? Yet one thing was certain. Despite the prediction that he might be one of the rare ones who died painfully, when the time came, the air at his bedside was "thick with peace."

Accepting someone's dying means letting her take the lead. The skillful caregiver yields in ways as graceful as ballet and almost as strenuous. One thinks of the willowlike strength developed through the martial arts, whose students learn to win by giving ground.

The martial art analogy is apt. We need the courage and commitment of a warrior to surrender to our patients, but it is precisely this profound acceptance that will change us. To be transformed by the experience, we must put aside our preconceptions of who we think they are—and who we think *we* are.

Caregiving constantly puts the caregiver's identity on the line. At the moment we learn of a loved one's terminal illness, the structure of our life gets shaken. Our minds leap to where the dying person fits in. The familiar patterns will be torn. When our lover is gone, who will put us first in their lives? When our child is gone, who will depend on us for survival? Without them, who are we?

We experience the loved one's impending loss of life as our loss of self. Because we mourn our death with theirs, we can honestly say, "I know how you feel." The sufferings of caregiver and care partner resonate like a pair of tuning forks.

This resonance is compassion, a word derived from the Latin meaning "suffering with." Compassion is not pity, which coldly distances us from others. In compassion we experience no distinction between ourselves and our patients. There is an effortless sense of generosity and joy as we each take care of the other. Truly compassionate people are a pleasure to be around.

"Suffering with" is the ground which gives rise to acceptance, but when we are too full of our own suffering, we can't accept the suffering of others. The grief that quite naturally accompanies caregiving can incapacitate. We should set grief aside as best we can while actually doing the work. As conscious caregivers we identify our patients' needs and our own, then choose to put theirs before ours.

Going from activity to activity—changing the sheets, giving a back rub, sitting quietly and saying nothing—we accept what each moment requires. "All that we should do is just do something as it comes," says Suzuki-roshi.[1] Whatever it takes: that's the liberating spirit of complete acceptance.

Devoting ourselves to the needs of others can free us from our own troubled thoughts and feelings. When I began doing hospice work, I was grieving the loss of a twenty-year marriage and separation from my two young sons, who had moved to Australia with my ex-wife. The agony was ongoing, but when I arrived to do my shift, I found I could leave my problems on the threshold. The patients' problems were so much greater than mine. In giving relief to them, I gave relief to myself.

Perhaps this is a selfish motivation for caregiving. The ego is part of everything we do. It can't be eliminated, but it can be brought into balance with awareness. We are mindful of the "me" in our caregiving so it doesn't overwhelm our work. Monitoring our thoughts and feelings, we stay awake to our responses at the bedside. What *are* our needs? If we are going to meet the needs of others, we must be mindful of our own.

Denying our needs can give rise to pretense. The caregiver who puts on a falsely cheerful face armors herself against experiencing emotion and cannot convey heartfelt support. Among the hospice volunteers I've worked with, those who smiled compulsively tended to quit before completing their commitment. Fear of their own feelings made the work too stressful. It was probably good that they left; dying people have an instinctive aversion to pretense. There just isn't time for it.

The more we can absent ourselves from our habitual ways of doing things, the more effective we will be. Caregiving requires us to be real. Always being "nice" is always being in control. Being real is a far riskier proposition. It requires that we meet our loved ones completely and respond without reservation. In this honest, wholehearted response there is the hope of transformation.

It's sometimes said in the helping professions that we must achieve self-acceptance before we can accept others; we must heal our own wounds before we can be healers. I disagree. Healing can be mutual. If we take care of the dying in a mindful way, they will take care of us. We just start where we are and feel our way. They tell us what they need, and we give them the best we can offer at every moment. This is how healing happens in all directions.

DON'T CATCH HELPER'S DISEASE

Many people become caregivers because they need to address their own inner needs and fears. This impulse is good; it arises from the desire for growth that is innate in all of us. But although wanting to change ourselves is good, wanting to change our patients is not.

Conscious caregivers are aware of their personal growth issues and don't let them subvert their caregiving. Compulsive caregivers suffer from Helper's Disease.

These are its symptoms:

✦ The need to be doing something constantly for the patient

✦ The belief that "altruism is good for you" and will produce "helper's high"

✦ A barely concealed tone of moral or religious superiority

✦ Always wanting to give and never receive

Those who suffer from Helper's Disease adopt a "do-gooder" stance that distances them from their patients and from themselves. The healthy alternative is bearing witness to the suffering of others while staying open to our own. The exchange is mutual. The care that is truly given is also truly received.

This requires both courage and restraint. It takes courage to be present for pain no matter what; it takes restraint to stay grounded in our own breath and not react in the habitual ways.

In letting go of a dying loved one, we must learn to let go of any special role as a helper. Genuine helping comes from the spirit; we are not the ones doing it. It just happens. We cannot resolve the tasks of dying people. We can only encourage them, with our love and attention, to meet their own challenges.

MAKING MISTAKES

So many big and little problems arise in the course of caregiving that we can't possibly do everything right. Mistakes happen. This is normal. Any time we deeply aspire to get engaged with life we become aware of our mistakes, because life includes both perfection and imperfection. Suzuki-roshi described the life of a master as "one continuous mistake."[2] This means it is one continuous act of accepting life as it is.

One of my most "continuous mistakes" occurs when I try to operate the power lifts on hospital beds. I always seem to be raising someone when I should be lowering him, or vice versa. Once I snagged the corner of a rising bed on a dangling cord from a table lamp and brought down not only the lamp but a tray full of food as well. What a mess!

I remember with appreciation how Joseph, a sweet-tempered man painfully dying of AIDS, reassured me each time my misuse of his bed jarred his sensitive nerves. "You're the best volunteer there is," he would say. "When they give the award, I vote for you."

Not every patient is so good-natured. There was a bank president who would ring his bedside bell for dinner at precisely 7:00 P.M. If his tray didn't arrive promptly, which it usually didn't, he showed his irritation with a deferential arch of his eyebrows. This subtle put-down amused volunteers, but it's not so funny when patient discontent escalates to full-blown rage.

Many dying people labor under a heavy load of anger. This is so common it may be a natural part of the letting-go process. When our less-than-perfect caregiving causes our patients to unload their anger on us, we are offered an opportunity. If we can accept anger without responding in kind, we strengthen our patience. And it strengthens our capacity to live more fully.

Patience is the endurance of threat. What we find threatening in others is often what we don't like in ourselves. The intimacy of hospice work encourages us to take down the walls and let life flow. In giving acceptance, we receive vitality.

Doing this again and again, cultivating the compassion of a grandmother, we become our own caregivers. We have to be kind to ourselves if we want to be kind to our patients. Helping others is a completely reciprocal process. Asked how we can help other people, my teacher, Mel Weitsman, replied, "Who is 'other people'? Help yourself."[3]

OBSTACLES TO ACCEPTANCE

It's pretty obvious that we withhold acceptance when we convey a negative judgment of someone's illness. Seeing the illness as God's punishment, or the result of bad karma, or bad diet, or bad attitude only add to the pain of the patient, and none of us want to do that. But we need to go beyond this good intention.

In order to do the work well, a caregiver has to be well informed about the disease process. If we don't understand what our patients are going through, we will have a harder time accepting their cognitive and physical limitations. When we learn how to interpret our patients, we encourage their trust and ease their pain of loneliness.

Professional home caregivers are the primary resource for questions about your loved one's illness. Keep a notebook handy to jot down your questions as they come up or use the Patient Log explained in the Home Skill section of Chapter 7. Then ask the visiting nurse. Educating caregivers is an important part of the nurse's job.

Another barrier to acceptance is expecting our loved one to recover. The day-to-day work of feeding, cleaning, and comforting a dying person tends to give rise to the unspoken hope that what we're doing will help them get better. Caring is not curing. We can improve the quality of our loved one's last days, but we can't prevent them from dying. If we harbor a hope of recovery, we may say things that make them uncertain as to whether or not they should be receiving palliative hospice care instead of curative medical treatment.

The opposite danger is expecting their death to occur "on schedule." Caregiving is hard work. If the person lives long past the prognosis, the caregiver can get trapped between wanting their life to go on and wanting the stress and fatigue of the work to be over. This painful ambivalence can cause anger and guilt in the caregiver, and it can make patients feel they aren't fulfilling expectations.

AIDS can be especially cruel in this regard. The virus gives rise to life-threatening illnesses that carry people through repeated cycles of collapse and recovery, exhausting the energy of both patient and caretakers. One person with AIDS told me it made him feel so guilty to keep putting his friends under stress that he was considering suicide.

It can be difficult to accept a dying person visibly damaged by the onslaught of serious illness. Instead of the familiar healthy form we knew as father or friend or lover we see frail limbs and gaunt features and we recoil in fright, rejecting the startling image of our own human impermanence.

Our patients perceive this instinctive pulling back as rejection. Dying people are keenly aware of the way society judges death a failure. They are especially sensitive to negative attitudes among friends and family. When we communicate our disapproval, we exacerbate our loved one's pain. When we extend our acceptance, we ease their pain.

Acceptance is a fast and effective pain reliever. It is also empowering. By conveying acceptance to our loved one we help them move past self-doubt and continue on to the new terrain at the end of life's journey. Acceptance is essential to growth. And in accepting our dying loved ones, we make it easier to let them leave. We can't let go of that which we do not accept as it is.

Perhaps the ugliest obstacle to acceptance is the practice of blaming patients for their own life-threatening illnesses. Human history has seen a lot of this particular cruelty, often as a result of misguided religious beliefs. In the present era, AIDS has evoked just such a blaming response from large parts of American society.

A more subtle form of this intolerance arises from New Age notions that see illness as "all in the mind." Implicit in this view is the notion that those who succumb to fatal disease are somehow inferior. We direct hurtful blaming at ourselves when we assume responsibility for our patients' conditions. Taking on another's pain is usually a way of avoiding our own, a symptom of Helper's Disease.

STAGES OF DYING

Another potential obstacle to accepting our patients as they are arises from too literally applying the influential "stages of dying" theory. This theory was formulated several decades ago by Dr. Elisabeth Kübler-Ross. She posited that people pass through five psychological stages of dying. These are denial, anger, bargaining to buy time (if I live I promise to . . .), depression, and, finally, acceptance.

The stages of dying theory suggests a great deal more uniformity in the way people die than I've actually seen. Among the dozens of people I've cared for, there has usually been a shocked denial at the beginning, peaceful acceptance at the end, and various kinds of resistance in between.

What seems to me significant is not the sequence of stages but rather the fact that the process points toward acceptance. We should find comfort in this, since peace is the end we desire for ourselves and our loved ones. Wanting them to rest in peace, we look for what we can do to help make it happen.

At the time she formulated her theory, Kübler-Ross suggested that we could help patients move past denial by bringing up the subject of their death when appropriate. Others have taken this to mean we should intervene at each stage to move people along. If our patient is stuck at anger, for example, we should encourage her to blow off steam so she can move on to the bargaining stage.

To push people to die in any particular way violates the hospice fundamental that everyone has the right to die his or her own way. Kübler-Ross certainly believed this. She conducted her research by simply letting dying people pour out their fears and concerns while she sat and listened.

It's a good model for us. If we want our patients to accept their death, we should accept their dying as it is. Acceptance is a highly effective treatment. Exactly how it works is cogently explained by one of Kübler-Ross's colleagues, Mwalimu Imara:

Going through the five stages of the terminal person's grief is a process moving toward a blessing, "acceptance." But we are able to journey fully through the process only when we feel the "acceptance" of another person. Our "acceptance" of our own being, that is, our sensing that we are significant as a person, depends on knowing that we are accepted by someone or something larger than our individual self. It is at this juncture that those who minister to the needs of the dying may become physicians to the soul.[4]

As "physicians to the soul," caregivers should adopt the guiding rule for all healers: it's better to do nothing than to intervene and make the situation worse. Don't push for anything. Expect nothing; accept everything. Our compassion naturally gives rise to wanting our loved ones' suffering to end, but the best way to help them let go of their lives is to give them the safety of our total acceptance.

Whether we hope our loved ones will live or hope they will die gracefully, our hope can be a barrier to accepting them just as they are. "Be still, and wait without hope," wrote T. S. Eliot in *Four Quartets*, "for hope would be hope for the wrong thing."

Waiting without hope is not hopelessness. It is finding optimism and satisfaction in what is here now. When we stop pushing our patients toward a special outcome, we discover the great possibilities that are present in the ordinary work of caregiving. Chop wood, carry water, admonishes the Zen saying. Change diapers, rub backs. And wait without hope.

"WHAT DOES MY PATIENT NEED?"

What is appropriate for a dying person today may not be appropriate tomorrow. We need to stay in touch at every point in the process.

People with terminal illness face multiple miseries, but despite their many discomforts, they may find it very hard to ask for help.

A strongly independent person may not want to acknowledge her new dependency. Emotional turmoil can render a normally articulate person speechless. Or there may be a physiological cause of cognitive impairment.

Don't assume you know what your patient wants. Always ask. An open-ended question ("Do you need anything?") may not help. Seriously ill people sometimes have difficulty discovering and expressing preferences.

Offer guiding questions: Would you like some classical music? A dish of chocolate ice cream? A foot massage? And don't take every response at face value. For example, if your loved one is always asking you to run off and do errands, it may be that what he really wants is for you to sit down and give him a little attention.

We had a wonderfully strong-willed West Indian woman in the hospice who had to be asked many times before she'd finally consent to coming to our Friday afternoon "happy hour." Perhaps her thirty years as a Sunday school teacher made her averse to attending an open bar party, but once she got there, she loved it. Another patient, a former merchant marine, would have us fix him a bedside hot toddy now and then. It was great to hang out and hear his tales from his travels. (Ah, the girls in Tahiti . . .) But sometimes he wanted to talk, and sometimes he just wanted to be alone with his drink and his memories. You had to check with him each time.

Getting down to what's really bothering someone may take a little time. We had an elderly gentleman named Frank who generally stayed burrowed under his covers with his eyes closed. One day he called me over and in a soft, husky voice asked me to massage his right knee. It was his only knee; his other leg had been amputated at the thigh. As I worked on Frank's kneecap he confessed he'd had so much pain the night before that he'd slept very little. When he said he was terribly afraid the pain would start again, I realized that it was the fear of pain that was bothering him more than the pain itself. But first I put an ice pack on his knee to ease the pain. Then I set out to ease his fear by using the comeditation technique of matching my breath to his and saying "aah" deeply each time he exhaled. (See the Home Skill at the end of Chapter 8.) In twenty minutes Frank was fast asleep and I was calm and refreshed.

It takes time to learn how to read patients' needs. In telling us what they need, patients use whatever means of communication are available to them. I've cared for Chinese, Japanese, and Polish patients who didn't speak a word of English. Others have been so confused by disease that their English was unintelligible. Listen with your ears and your eyes. Body language is a tip-off. "Please rub my back between the shoulder blades," for example, might be expressed with a twitching of the shoulders and a faintly irritated expression.

Silence is also a valid response. One of the more reclusive patients got so disgusted with our always asking him what he wanted that he took to wearing a baseball cap emblazoned with the words "Leave Me Alone." We got it!

As you study your patient, also study yourself. What you are saying in word and action? Seek to embody acceptance. Convey it through slow movements and careful speech. Before you do a bedside procedure like changing the sheets, gently lay your hand on your loved one's arm and then explain what you are going to do.

Take requests seriously. Things that might not seem significant to you can be very meaningful to your patient. Feeling a need for control in the face of growing helplessness, she might find comfort in having with her small things that hold big memories, like a beloved teddy bear or an old blanket. Honor these requests as best you can, and look for other ways to spoil your loved ones. If her favorite color is blue, buy her a blue nightgown. If he is a sports fan, read him *Sports Illustrated*.

When health permits, excursions to restaurants, theaters, clubs, and sporting events are a great morale booster. Federal regulations requiring access for the disabled have opened doors to the dying, but you still have to check the logistics. Are there comfortable chairs? Will the air-conditioning make a sweater necessary? Where are the bathrooms? Should you sit by the door? And of course you should never promise more than you can deliver. Be realistic, but don't be afraid to think big. Help your loved one dream up something wonderful, and see if there's a way to make it happen. These wish trips can express deep longings that need resolution.

Excursions don't have to be a big deal. Just getting outside for fresh air can be an exciting experience for someone feeling cooped up. If going out isn't possible, plan special occasions at home. Organize a bedside dinner party or have a choral group come in from church or bring friends in to play cards. Everything depends on your patient's health and preferences. Some people find arts and crafts like modeling with clay or drawing and coloring less tiring than reading or talking or watching television.

Whatever you offer, let it arise from the patient's needs, not yours. Guard against compulsiveness. If your loved one loses interest in an activity you oh-so-carefully organized, give it up gracefully. Caregiving is intimate work that requires us to adapt to the person in our care. This can really test our limits. Some of the hardest hospice work I ever did was to accompany a man who spent most of his last days watching TV soap operas. It was simply awful, but at least he didn't channel-surf.

The dying father of my friend Darlene Cohen wouldn't stay on any one TV channel for more than forty-five seconds except at news time. Then he clicked wildly between news shows. Darlene found herself yearning for the completion of even the most insipid dialogue. "The heroine would say something like 'I can't see you again unless you give up stock car racing,'" says Darlene, who can find the humor in anything, "and I would gasp as my dad clicked away her lover's reply. It was pretty interesting watching how attached I was to continuity," she says. "*Any* continuity."

Watching TV probably wasn't on your agenda when you set out

to do hospice work as a spiritual practice, but the pilgrim's path traverses much dull terrain. This is the big omission in all those books about *Zen and the Art of. . . .* Yes, the master archer is able to hit the bull's-eye without looking, but only after years and years of boring, repetitive practice.

Stay attentive to your patient and don't let your mind wander to wishing for more "spiritually significant" work. The work's significance reveals itself as you identify what has to be done and then devote your full attention to the task, no matter how mundane it might be. But always, in everything you do, be willing to settle for doing your best. Don't demand a perfection that excludes imperfection. It doesn't exist. Nature simply doesn't work that way.

Home Skill: Forming a Support Group

The support group shares the responsibility of caregiving among many people. It provides practical services and emotional support for the dying person and for its own members.

To form a support group, the person who is dying should draw up a list of people from whom she would want to receive help. People to consider are close friends; family members, including children; neighbors; coworkers; and friends from religious organizations or social groups.

The person's partner or closest friend or relative should call those on the list, explain the purpose of the support group, and ask them to join. (In most cases the caller will be person's primary caregiver.) Invite an honest response; it's best if lack of commitment surfaces early. The dying person needs support from people who really want to be there.

Those willing to serve should meet together. Agenda items for this meeting are identifying who can do what, deciding how often to meet as a group, and making a phone list of members from which a phone tree can be constructed. The phone tree is a system of relay-

ing information by calling the person immediately in front of you on
your branch.

Organizing the first meeting should be the job of someone whose
time isn't taken by patient care. Potluck dinners are good because
they invite involvement by everyone and encourage a mood of
neighborliness, but don't make food the focus of the meeting. Start
with a short period of meditation to set a deeper tone. Then have
all present say a few words about themselves and ask whatever
questions they might have. Go on to discuss the patient's needs
and how to meet them. Assign someone to help with the following:

—Direct patient care
—Night care
—Occasional companionship
—Emergency support
—Housekeeping
—Shopping
—Laundry
—Child care
—Pet care
—Financial planning
—Legal affairs (wills, powers of attorney)
—Advocacy with social service agencies
—Funeral planning
—Medical research
—Transportation, including car maintenance
—Returning phone calls
—Procuring medical supplies and equipment
—General errands
—Hosting out-of-town visitors

It may not be possible to assign all these tasks at the first meeting,
but they need to be addressed soon. Some people will gravitate toward emotional tasks; others will prefer doing practical things.

Everyone should be encouraged to state his or her personal limits, and these preferences should be respected. But no one should feel the need to be an "expert." Everyone has the compassion it takes to care for another person and to do it well.

Although caregiving is a work of the heart in which all, including the children, can share, the hands-on care of feeding, medicating, turning to prevent bedsores, and assisting elimination is rarely done by all family members. Some may have qualms about doing perineal care (care of the genitals) and about coping with incontinence. This is understandable, but doing the work will generate a tender love that overcomes fear and revulsion.

Support group members should meet together occasionally as a "family." Adding a meeting to the already crowded caregiving calendar may seem like too much, but coming together makes the load easier to bear. Everyone gets a chance to share the latest news on the loved one's health, exchange bedside experiences, and voice difficult feelings about death and loss, thus making these feelings easier to understand and accept.

If the terminal condition lingers, family meetings may stretch over many months, or even years. But even if there's time for only a few meetings, they can clarify feelings, create a sense of common purpose, and bring the reality of death more sharply into focus. The wisdom of group discussion deepens the quality of patient care and opens the hearts of caregivers.

The support group should continue to meet after the loved one has died to extend bereavement support to its members.

Ongoing support groups can be found through many national organizations for specific diseases and through local social service agencies.

Six

Giving the Gift of Listening

Human beings are peculiar because
all they have to do is talk about their
distress and they feel better.

—Dr. Derek Kerr

THREE MONTHS AFTER I BEGAN DOING hospice work, I longed to do more than I could as a volunteer. I was an important part of the caregiving team, but I had no medical training. It seemed to me that if I were a doctor or nurse I could better address the needs of dying patients.

This thought weighed on my mind for weeks. Finally I went to the library and pored over medical school catalogs. It was obvious that someone my age with a family couldn't manage the time and money required. It seemed I'd missed my calling.

I was feeling glum when I showed up for my next hospice shift. It didn't help that I started out working with Adele, an old Russian woman with hawkish eyes who was usually pretty glum herself. As I walked into her room she appeared especially tense and out of sorts. Expecting the worst I planted myself by her bed and asked what I could do. "Sit down," Adele said, glaring out from under her eyebrows. "Sit down and shut up." This woman really knew what she wanted. It made me laugh. Then she started grinning, and for the next hour we sat pleasantly immersed in the quiet intimacy that had settled over the room. When I left, she was asleep and I felt quite rested.

Mulling over the incident later, I realized that Adele had answered my question. I knew what I could do that doctors and nurses couldn't. They were busy, but I had plenty of time. I could give patients my undivided attention. I could sit down and shut up. And I could listen.

There is no caregiving tool more valuable than listening. It's amazing how much "merely listening" can accomplish.

Nearly every hospice has stories about people who arrived with one foot in the grave only to flourish in the hospice environment. I think it's the listening. Caregivers know how to heal pain by listening to it.

Listening heals through the power of generosity. The listener devotes, offers, gives full attention to the speaker. The gift is openhanded and expects nothing in return. It is charity in the ancient sense—not philanthropy but love. Like real love, real listening simply makes itself a part of what's going on. In true listening, as in true love, we become one.

This requires letting go. In truly listening we are willing to be changed by what we hear. We don't try to steer the conversation. We abandon our resistance, relinquish control, and stop guarding our feelings. We step out from behind our defenses and share with our patients a free exchange from which everyone benefits.

The gift of listening enriches the giver. Learning how to give is an essential step on the spiritual path because generosity opens the heart and sustains it on the journey. The generous listener both gives and receives the abundance of life.

TALKING ABOUT DYING

Death is so socially repressed in our culture that many terminally ill people broach the topic in a roundabout way, if at all. Some wait, weary and frightened, for their lives to be over without ever sharing the agony. Others live out their last days uncertain they are actually dying.

Doctors and relatives used to decide whether or not to disclose to a dying person the news of a terminal illness. The consumer health movement of the 1970s successfully claimed that patients had a right to know. These days some doctors wait for the patient to ask, or disclose voluntarily only when shifting the patient from curative to palliative care, but most doctors disclose most of the time.

Honesty is generally the best policy. The truth hurts, but usually it doesn't hurt as much as uncertainty. Keeping death secret only makes it more fearsome and adds to the pain of dying. Leo Tolstoy's great short story, "The Death of Ivan Illich" describes this anguished uncertainty. Eventually Ivan Illich intuits the severity of his illness, and most dying people do the same.

Patients who are not told of their diagnosis but know anyway that they are dying may fall into helplessness. Those who can openly discuss their situation with others have a much better chance of being able understand and accept its finality. By establishing a good listening relationship, we lay the groundwork for them to plan for their incapacity and death through **advance directives** that clearly establish their preferences.

The following are practical issues that must be addressed while the dying person is still cogent:

✦ A **durable power of attorney for health care** designates a person to make health care decisions should the patient become incapacitated.

✦ A **living will** directs medical personnel to withhold specified life-sustaining equipment and treatments when the person becomes irreversibly unconscious. The living will prevents the unnecessary prolongation of life made possible by new medical technologies.

Note: In many states the person given health care power of attorney can override the provisions of a living will. It's a good idea to have both documents anyway. Writing the will is a good way for the dying person to clarify her preferences. These should include how she wants her terminal pain treated as well as which meditation tapes, readings, music, and scriptures she wants read or played while she is unconscious.

✦ A list of people the patient would like to have nearby in his final hours will help the dying person to envision a peaceful death.

✦ Details of the memorial service are a great help to family and friends wanting to do what their loved one would desire.

✦ A statement of what the patient wants done with his or her body after death, including whether organs may be donated, helps avoid difficult questions later.

Sometimes dying people who want to talk about their condition encounter resistance from family and friends. Never say, "Don't talk about that now." If your loved one seems to want to talk about dying, don't let the daily demands of caregiving prevent you. Discussing the patient's impending death is important for you, too, because doing so helps you work through your own fear and grief.

Look for an opening, and when it occurs, offer the topic in language that is comfortable to your loved one. If she would prefer a disguised or symbolic discourse, speak in those terms. If he is reluctant to enter into a direct dialogue, it may be because he is trying to shield you. In this case your open acknowledgment of the death will make it easier.

Truth telling should be balanced against how much truth the person wants to hear. Neither reject nor reinforce denial. If your loved one wants to talk about getting better ("As soon as I get up I'm going to . . .") acknowledge her aspirations ("Yes, it would be fun to . . .") without supporting her in denial.

Respect the truth by saying only what you know about dying and death. Support your loved one in his struggle with fear by acknowledging that you don't have all the answers. Don't keep hope alive with false promises, and don't kill it, either. Long-term remission of illness or even miraculous recovery can never be ruled out.

Dr. Elisabeth Kübler-Ross, whose unflagging commitment to the truth made her the founder of modern thanatology, advises caregivers not to volunteer information but to answer all questions honestly. In this view patients will ask for the bad news when they're ready for it. If they never ask, it's not an error. It's their choice, and we need to respect it, even if it means we don't achieve the closure we so desperately want.

In walking the fine line between telling or not telling people about their death, caregivers should always err on the side of compassion. In most cases this means telling the truth, but there are exceptions. Although dying is an ordinary event, it is also a personal catastrophe. Even great masters give up their lives with reluctance.

LIFE REVIEW

Our minds tend toward a sense of completion. When we reach the end of our lives, we want to close the circle by coming to terms with the people, events, and possessions most important to us.

A dying person may spend long hours sorting through mementos, photo albums, and old letters; in phone conversations with long-lost friends and relatives; and in solitary contemplation. This life review is not an exercise in autobiography but rather an inquiry into meaning. We review our lives to make sense of them.

The way dying people move toward synthesis reflects who they are. Methodical people may sort through their years like librarians, putting thoughts and experiences in place like books on a shelf. Talkers may just want to reminisce. Artistic types may prefer to work intuitively. Modeling with clay or drawing with colored pencils can help them link up with their memories.

David Wells, a stage designer, used artwork to articulate and understand his identity. His crayon drawings of dream and comic-book images expressed the moods and feelings that had possessed and inspired him throughout his life. His art became a medium of confession, catharsis, and, ultimately, purification. When he died he radiated an almost saintly sense of forgiveness.

In dying we judge ourselves, and in telling our stories we seek self-forgiveness. Caregivers can aid patients' self-forgiveness through positive listening. In positive listening, we identify and gently feed back the ways our loved ones have overcome obstacles in their lives. This helps them accept and be grateful for the people, events, and places that shaped who they are.

Dying people often forget how many problems they have successfully handled. Seeing the heroism in their own life stories will help them summon up the strength to cope with the problems life presents as it comes to an end.

Self-acceptance can't be rigged, however. Our job as caregivers is to help our loved ones work through the complexity and ambiguity of their lives as they are. We should resist any temptation to manipulate their stories to make them conclude with happy endings. Authenticity is essential. "We make ourselves real by telling the truth," Thomas Merton wrote.[1]

The truth is not always the facts. As listeners we don't correct the record, we encourage further inquiry. Much of who we are is hidden from us. In digging, we don't know what will come to light or how it will be received. Sensing judgment in the listener, we censor ourselves. Instead of speaking the truth, we speak what seems acceptable. When others hear and accept us as we really are, we are likely to dig deeper.

A practical tip: Dying people want to feel useful; recording their life stories will let them feel they are passing on what they've learned to future generations. A tape recorder or video camera can be used to capture their messages. However, their most revealing statements are likely to come when the recording device is turned off and they feel free to talk "off the record."

FINAL EMOTIONAL TASKS

In delving into their lives, dying people encounter emotional problems that need to be solved so they can rest in peace. Life review brings into focus old wrongs that demand reconciliation and old wounds that want healing.

These are vital needs. When patients can express them, caregivers should make every effort to facilitate resolution.

If your loved one wants to visit old familiar places or meet with people out of the past, try to fulfill these requests. If a difficult letter needs to be written and the patient is too weak to write it, tape-record what he wants to say and send the cassette in lieu of a letter. If a financial debt troubles her, help find a way to pay it. If she wants reassurance that loved ones can get along without her, provide it.

Listen to understand what your patient wants to accomplish. Anything you can do to help a loved one untie old knots of guilt and lay to rest troubling fantasies will aid him to affirm that although he might have done things better in life, he did the best he could. The anxious, agitated patient whose dying drags on may be delaying until these issues are resolved and this assurance is secured.

Often a patient's deep issues do not surface in clear and coherent requests. Eric Poché, a professional caregiver, says patients are always trying to tell us their truth, but they aren't sure they can trust us so they communicate in ways that aren't obvious. When you ask your loved one if she has any unfinished business, be alert for the subtle ways in which the answer is communicated.

When you have a confusing or intense exchange, it may mean that something is trying to surface. Take a moment to review what happened. Write it down so you can talk it over with hospice staff and with your family or support group. Let collective wisdom guide you in understanding what your loved one might be trying to say. Then determine how you can help him say it in a way that will increase his sense of well-being and ease his passing.

THE MIND OF LISTENING

In good listening we listen in two directions: outwardly to our patient, and inwardly to our own thoughts and feelings. When we line up how we feel with what we say and do, we communicate in a genuine and believable way.

Listening to ourselves teaches awareness. We discover that the mind produces thoughts much faster than the patient can produce words. This makes us impatient. We find ourselves drifting into daydreams or wanting to break in on what she is saying. We want to pass judgments, probe, cross-examine, inject advice, or change the subject. We want to push our opinions when all that's needed is acceptance.

All of this happens in the head; we don't have to act on it. Instead, we just "let our mud settle" and return our attention again and again to our patients. We remind ourselves to listen in the same way we remind ourselves to come back to our breath in meditation. The listening mind is very similar to the broadly focused, yet keenly alert mind cultivated through meditation.

THE HEART OF LISTENING

Good listening is similar to meditation but not quite so dispassionate. The good listener does not coolly observe but rather warmly resonates. This sympathetic vibration is the interpersonal experience we call empathy.

Listening is the heart of our work as caregivers, and empathy is the heart of our listening.

Empathy is much more powerful than sympathy. Sympathy is feeling sorry for another person. Empathy is feeling that person's experience as if it were our own. One thinks of the primitive custom of *couvade*, in which the husband takes to his bed while his wife is giving birth and imitates her labor and childbirth.

Of course the husband cannot actually feel what his wife is experiencing. Each of us is unique, and our individual experiences are nontransferable. But although we can't penetrate other people, we can understand intimately what they are going through by finding its equivalent in ourselves. We tune in to them by tuning in to ourselves. We share their experience *as if* it were ours because their thoughts, motives, and feelings are deeply familiar to us.

In order to feel another's experience we have to feel our own. We meet our loved ones at the emotional depth we reach in ourselves. We know their joy, sadness, and pain as deeply as we know our own. We listen to them as fully as we are willing to listen to ourselves.

The risks are great, but so are the rewards. Empathetic listening creates the conditions for wise understanding. We think our best strategy in life is self-defense. Through empathetic listening we discover that the opposite is true. Although we are each unique, we are at the same time joined together.

This paradoxical nature of being alive is summed up in the saying "Not one, not two." Acts of empathy express our innate desire to overcome the "oneness" of our isolation and honor the "twoness" of relationship.

Seeking to identify with the feelings of our patients enlarges our sense of who we are. As we open our hearts, the walls of our isolated kingdoms crumble. Knowing that we are not alone, or even separate, we feel tremendous relief.

BETTER LISTENING TECHNIQUES

Doctors and nurses are trained to listen to patients in order to properly treat their symptoms. This is listening for information, a skill that caregivers develop in the course of their work. Watch for changes in your patient's physical condition: feverish temperature, altered breathing, or a slow or rapid pulse might require action. Don't hesitate to call the hospice nurse or doctor any time you become concerned about a change.

The listening of caregivers unearths much useful information, but it penetrates below this level. The caregiver's real work is to establish connection so the patient can reveal what needs to be shared. Let go of any pressure to fix problems or answer questions or resolve disputes and listen. Just listen.

As you're rushing around the house taking care of tasks, stop by now and then to touch your loved one with a warm word and a soft hand. These quick visits communicate your concern, but they don't establish empathy. Budget definite times when you'll have the energy to listen with full attention. Try to make these times fit with the patient's rhythms for eating, sleeping, bathing, and companionship. Night is often difficult for dying people, so that's a good time to offer a sympathetic ear.

Better listening begins at the moment you approach your patient's bed. Set aside your busyness, and take a deep breath. Check how you feel inside at that moment. Check your patient. Does she look like she wants to talk? Appearances can be deceiving. Patients with eyes closed and heads buried in their covers may perk right up when there's a chance to converse. Others who appear open and alert may turn away. Don't be offended when this happens. Dying people need lots of private time.

Study gestures, postures, and facial expressions to understand your loved one's true feelings. As a nonprofessional you may not catch all the nuances, but you can probably identify the patterns. What actions typically accompany his words? Does silence usually mean she wants to be left alone? Or is she making a silent cry for attention?

Always initiate any conversation by asking your loved one if he wants to talk. If he signals, either verbally or nonverbally, that he does, sit down so your eyes are on the same level as his. Get close enough to connect without encroaching on the patient's "personal zone"—about two feet away is usually best.

Relax and let your body language show it. Remember that your patient is watching you. (Most people gather information visually.) An erect, settled posture communicates interest, openness, and a commitment to stay put and listen.

+ Keep your head up and your back straight.

+ Slide your bottom well back in the chair and rest your weight on the "sitting bones."

+ Put your hands on the arms of the chair or, if it has no arms, in your lap.

+ Keep your feet flat on the floor with your legs uncrossed.

Correct posture may seem like too much to ask from a tired caregiver badly in need of slouching down for a few minutes' rest, but the patient longs to be heard, and your full attention can help this happen. Bharat J. Lindemood, a counselor at Shanti Project, writes: "Working with hospitalized patients, how I feel is often directly correlated with what happens. When I am feeling centered and open, we often have long in-depth sessions. When I am tired or shut down, suddenly they all seem to be taking naps."[2]

Employ all your senses. Listen with your eyes, hands, nose, and sometimes even with your mouth. (A kiss can tell a lot.)

As you sit by your friend or loved one, mentally step back into the big picture. When you adopt a broad state of mind you can create a safe and private space at the bedside. Listening from a stance that is expansive and open creates a warm, personal, and encouraging presence that is not intrusive.

Remember that a terminally ill person can be very sick and very fragile. Adopt a clear, unthreatening gaze that encourages talk. Make your patient, rather than the illness, the focus of the conversation. Help her unload what's on her mind by repeating back a little bit of what she's just said. Feedback lets your loved one know you are listening and confirms that you got it right. If she raises difficult issues she needs to resolve for herself, help her find her own answers by asking what she thinks.

FREEDOM OF SPEECH

There is nothing that cannot be said by a dying person, and there is no special way to say it. Let your loved one speak his truth in any way he chooses. Genuine listening is acceptance.

Dying people are wary of having to pretend to be something they aren't. Don't ask them to be polite or cheerful. The raw reality of their situation can make social fictions intolerable. If black humor is your loved one's way of coping, don't try to cheer her up with lighthearted jokes. Laughing to keep from crying is a valid way to ventilate grief and accept death.

Playing the "bad patient" is valid. Don't attempt to talk your patient out of negative feelings. Trust the process. It may be hard to believe, but arguing, complaining, confronting, and demanding can be growth affirming. Open your listening and make it a container for whatever needs to be said. Surrender to the situation. The good listener gives up in order to give.

Don't be afraid of silences. If your loved one stops talking it doesn't mean the dialogue is over; communication continues even when the words end. Share this poignant interlude outside the pressure of time. Silence may mean he is struggling with deep feelings. Let the silence fade like the sound of a bell, and, when you feel the moment is over, give an encouraging touch. If it seems appropriate, ask what your loved one was thinking.

Deep, empathetic listening helps others articulate difficult feelings. It opens to dying people a path through anger and fear to a place of safety and security—our listening presence. If they feel very secure they may tell us, and thus put in order, their unfinished business.

The good listener is unobtrusive, attentive, and lovingly efficient, but nobody can be good all the time. A caregiver doesn't have to be perfect. Accepting our not-so-good listening helps us to accept our patients. The less energy we expend in pushing away what we don't like about ourselves, the more we will have for our patients. When you hear a critical voice, let it have its say. And go on listening.

DEMENTIA

Almost every dying person experiences some degree of mental confusion caused by the distraction, fatigue, grief, and stress inherent in the process. Terminal illness and medications can further impair a person's capacity to think and speak clearly. Difficulty with concentration and the inability to remember several details at once are common. If mental confusion deepens into persistent disorientation, the person may be experiencing dementia.

Dementia is a progressive deterioration of intellectual function caused by brain cell damage. It results from small blood vessel hemorrhages, viral infections (as in AIDS-related dementia), tumor or cancer metastases, alcoholism, vitamin deficiencies, or many other causes specific to various diseases.

Dementia has behavioral consequences. Typically demented people experience memory lapses, have difficulty with language, lack good judgment and spatial perception, and give the impression of not being present. They may fall into depression, lose interest in life, and withdraw into passivity. They may get anxious, suspicious, and easily irritated. They may become delirious and call out for help or attempt to climb over the bed rails. As dying approaches and the body supplies less oxygen to the brain, they may become restless and agitated. They may not recognize you, or may see someone or something you don't. People with dementia often suffer a loss of motor control. They may have difficulty walking or roll too close to the edge of the bed, making safety a concern. As dementia advances, incontinence becomes likely.

Dementia is a common experience in dying, but that doesn't make it any easier to bear. A person's inability to find the right word can trigger a demeaning response from others. Getting lost in a memory maze can be frightening. Dementia can make us think we're going crazy, but it's not true. A dying person's dementia is not mental illness, and it's not a failure. It is a normal part of the process. Nor does it detract from a person's integrity. Despite Descartes's famous dictum ("I think, therefore I am"), humans are much more than their thoughts.

If your loved one's illness progresses to dementia, or if he is very close to death and appears unconscious, you are called upon to listen with even greater sensitivity. "Reading" a person in a nonverbal way can be a very rewarding experience. People who become demented have a lot to teach us about the difference between the person and the personality. With an open heart we can always love the deeper being that exists in every human.

People with dementia need reassurance. Give plenty of touch and frequent hugs, warm smiles, and direct eye contact. Soften your focus, open your senses wide, and connect through the heart. Your heartfelt concern can improve their communication; attention is an active ingredient.

Use simple words and calm, confident tones to reduce the risk of startling your loved one. If appropriate, you might ask questions to clarify and understand her feelings and point of view, but do more listening than talking. Reduce your side of the conversation to offering affirmative expressions like "yes" or "uh-huh" to show support and keep things moving. This doesn't mean you agree with everything that's being said. Even though we listen closely we may not be able to understand a thing our patients are saying. Remember, in hospice work listening is mostly a matter of being there.

Words are only the outer layer of what we're all about. Commit yourself to staying connected. In working with patients who appear to be unresponsive, remember that even people who are asleep or unconscious can still hear at some level, so speak carefully in their presence.

People with dementia need you to make their tangled world less confusing and frightening. Structure it for them. Put in the room a calendar and a clock with a sweep second hand. Keep a small blackboard by the bed, and write on it the day and your name or the names of visitors. Have your loved one name the food on the tray or the objects in the room, and give prompts when she gets stuck. For example, you point at the water and say: "a glass of ——." Touch is grounding. Give your loved one things to hold that are of different textures, such as a furry teddy bear, a piece of ice, or modeling clay.

People with dementia think in slow motion. Don't give them too much to process. When initiating a conversation, always identify yourself. Say what day and time it is. Speak of familiar names, places, and experiences. Build the conversation around photos of family members, friends, and pets. Visitors are helpful. People who are not able to speak still need normal social interaction, but too many voices can be confusing. Avoid large groups.

When performing patient care, give reasons for everything you do and explain step by step as you go. When you need the patient's help to do a task, such as changing position in bed, cue him with a "one, two, three, go" signal. Use your hands to guide him.

For more tips on how to work with a person with dementia see the Home Skill section at the end of the chapter. "Video Respite," listed in Appendix 1: Resources, is a series of videotapes that will stimulate and entertain people with dementia while their caregivers take a break.

THE HEART AND THE BELLY

Empathetic listening comes from an open heart, but keeping the heart open to dying people can be difficult. The swirl of feelings set off by their suffering can overcome and exhaust the listener who is "all heart."

One common strategy is to escape from our strong feelings by fleeing up into our minds. Looking down from the safety of our thoughts disconnects us from threatening emotions, but it also elevates us to a place of watching rather than listening. This is the place where medical professionals go when they distance themselves from their patients. The result is the physician who smiles warmly as he tells you your cancer is terminal.

As caregivers our intention is to stay close and connected to our loved ones. How can we keep our hearts in our work without being overcome by it? The answer is found not by escaping into our heads but by dropping our attention to the body center, the lower belly.[3]

Eastern spiritual traditions identify several centers in the body that shape our consciousness, and the belly is one of them. Energy flows through these centers, or chakras, where it is transformed and redistributed to the whole.

Through yoga and contemplation, specific chakras can be accessed to unleash their special energies. The region of the solar plexus, located about one inch below the navel, contains the chakra holding a wellspring of calm, stable strength.

Our culture acknowledges this strength when we say someone "has guts," but there is more power in the belly than mere intestinal fortitude. The martial arts are built on this principle. The frail master archer can easily bend a mighty bow by finding his strength in the belly. "You must realize that the center of the universe is the pit of your belly!" declared Sogaku Harada, one of the great contemporary masters.[4]

Belly has a bad rap in America. We are taught from childhood to suck in our stomachs and stick out our chests to conform to the top-heavy ideal personified by the Marine sergeant and the Playboy bunny. But as a caregiver you will greatly benefit from learning how to drop your mind's eye to your lower belly and do your caregiving from there.

Working from the head, we are coldly dispassionate, and our patients feel pitied rather than loved. Working from the heart, we exude love, but love without strength is dangerous; we may get needy and helpless. When we are strongly rooted in our bellies, we are much more likely to do the appropriate thing. Settling our work in the solar plexus give us a great deal of support for staying open and available to a dying person who is afraid and in pain.

The best listening engages both the heart and the belly. It's a two-step process. First, we tune in to the feelings of the person who's speaking—we make a heart connection by letting our feelings resonate with his. Second, we drop down and listen from the belly. When the mind is anchored there, it supports the heart, and we can respond to our patients' strong emotions with calm understanding and acceptance.

Here is how to do it:

1. Sit at the bedside in the upright way described on page 99. Keep your head up, your back straight, your bottom well back in the chair, your arms resting at your sides or in your lap, and your feet flat on the floor so that the knees are not higher than the hipbones.

2. Think of your lower belly and your buttocks as one solid thing, and let this solid base bear the weight of your upper body.

3. Drop your shoulders. This does not mean press them down. Release your shoulders completely and let them be pulled down by the weight of your arms.

4. Relax everything above the navel and breathe from the pit of your belly.

5. Let your patient completely fill the foreground of your attention while you settle your busy background mind on your breath as it rises and falls in the belly. And listen, listen and accept.

To test the effectiveness of listening from the belly, Dale Borglum, director of the Living/Dying Project, has people who attend his workshops pair up and try it out on each other. One person talks about something painful while the other "drops down" and listens from the belly. Dale calls this an exercise in empowerment.

Listening from the belly empowers us to accept the pain of others, and it empowers others to express their pain to us because they sense that we won't be overwhelmed. This is an important practice that lets difficult truths get said.

It may not be possible for your dying loved one to tell her whole truth before the time for truth telling ends. Be ready to accept that death has the last word. Or does it?

Although each of us is unique, we are all part of a larger life that makes itself known through our distinct, individual existences. As your dying loved one approaches the end of his story, listen closely and you may hear the existence that echoes endlessly.

Home Skill: Talking with the Neurologically Impaired

The following suggestions are drawn from research done by the Institute of Physical Medicine and Rehabilitation in Peoria, Illinois.

Keep conversation simple.

Speak slowly and in a matter-of-fact way.
Give the person plenty of time to respond.
Present only one idea at a time.

Encourage success in communication.

Take what the person says seriously; be generous with approval.
Support efforts to talk. If she forgets what she's saying, repeat her initial phrase as a prompt. For example, if she gets stuck on "I want to . . . ," repeat these words verbatim.
If the person gets stuck in a rambling thought, change the subject.
Don't ask questions that pose choices. Instead ask affirmative questions, such as, "Do you want a drink?" Or ask questions that require a pointing response: "Where is your teddy bear?"
Encourage talking with the hands by making gestures as you speak.

Avoid causing embarrassment.

Don't tease, put the person on display, or force him to speak.
Don't assume that difficulty in speaking means diminished intellect.
Speak as you would to any reasoning adult; never speak down.
Don't raise your voice. Hearing loss does not normally accompany neurological impairment.
Don't laugh at the person. If her dementia causes her to say

something funny and you laugh, make it a shared joke by explaining what you found funny.

Stay real.

Don't recoil from any raw expression of emotion.

Avoid false optimism or empty phrases.

Don't act as if you understand when you don't. Simply give an affirming but noncommittal "uh-huh."

Don't try to share hallucinations. Stay grounded. (On the other hand, imaginary visualizations of a trip to Waikiki or a night at La Scala can be fun and relaxing!)

Seven

The Tao of Eating and Elimination

It flows through all things, inside and outside,
and returns to the origin of all things.
                              —Tao Te Ching

Food is life. Thus the world's great religions incorporate food into their rituals. As we become intimate with the bodily processes of dying people, something like an earthy sense of sanctity arises. Helping them eat and use the toilet connects us with the universal body of all beings. This excerpt from my journals illustrates how dramatic this connection can be.

Lawrence, a very dignified man, must get to the toilet—*now*. The commode is only a few feet from his bed, but that's a long way to travel. Lawrence is paralyzed from the waist down.

Hurrying to help him, I jam on a pair of latex gloves and start to slide his legs over the edge of the bed. Then I notice that his catheter tube runs way over to a urine collection bag on the other side of the bed. The bag is stuck there. Someone, probably a new volunteer, wedged it between the mattress and the far bed rail when the bag was empty. Now it's full. If I squeeze too hard trying to get the bag out, it'll burst. But I have to get the bag out because Lawrence is connected to it and Lawrence has to move.

I ask Lawrence if he can wait while I drain the bag. He says he'll try, but as I'm down the hall getting a basin I hear him ringing his bell like crazy. His bowels have failed him. He's crapped on himself and the bed. He feels terrible about it.

No problem, I say; just let me empty this bag and I'll clean up the sheets. He says he can't wait. There's more on the way. Lawrence has to get to the toilet—*now.*

Feeling desperate, I try to wiggle out the jammed urine bag. As I push and pull I imagine myself slipping and sliding on a floor wet with piss from a burst catheter bag while I change a bed full of shit from his bowel movement. But the bag doesn't burst. So now I can ease Lawrence to his feet and out of the bed and somehow we manage to get over to the commode together. Then comes the hard part. I have pull down his shorts—full of excrement—without getting both of us covered. Done. He sits down, and together we give a big sigh.

Now he's slumped on the commode. I know his paralysis makes bowel movements arduous, so I put a pillow on the bed and have him lean forward and rest his head on it as a way of getting more comfortable. His soiled sheets need changing, but instead I decide to leave him in privacy.

My job is over; the rest is up to Lawrence. At the door I turn back and ask if everything's OK. "Perfect," he says. The guy is dying of AIDS, covered in shit, and everything is just perfect. The funny thing is, he means it.

EATING

DON'T PUSH FOOD OR DRINK

Since food is life, dying people tend to need less of it as body systems shut down and life diminishes. Toward the end they may want nothing except liquids. In the final days or hours, digestion usually quits completely, and they want nothing at all.

It can be hard to accept this natural process. We instinctively want to nurture our loved ones with food. Seeing them eat little or nothing, we feel a desperate urge to help. We know that without nourishment they will die, and we fear their death because we fear our own. So we push them to eat.

Never pressure a terminal patient to eat or drink. Eating won't prevent your loved one from dying. Her lack of appetite is not an eating disorder. If she wants little to eat, don't be alarmed. Think of it as a purifying fast for the journey ahead.

The hope that eating will make the dying person well can be hard to give up, especially in families where mealtimes traditionally serve to hold people together. A family member's lack of appetite can be seen as a threat. Family and friends should be a source of support at mealtimes, not a source of stress. Having company can encourage a bedridden person to eat by easing loneliness, but sometimes eating is simply impossible. And sometimes loneliness is necessary. Like everything in hospice, "it all depends."

Accepting our loved ones' lack of appetite doesn't mean we are indifferent to it. We should watch for any thought that what our patients eat doesn't matter because they are "going to die anyway." As caregivers we want our loved ones to live out every bit of life that is rightfully theirs. Eating can help them do it.

Dying people want to eat well. They believe that eating can make them feel better. They worry about their erratic appetite, and they know it makes others worry. These worries can be addressed, but the lack of appetite may be irremediable.

The disease process, and the medications and treatments that accompany it, can wreak havoc on the whole digestive tract—mouth to throat to stomach to bowels. For example, tumors in the stomach or pancreas can cause a feeling of fullness that dulls the taste buds. Liver tumors can make almost everything taste bad.

Even when a dying person has an appetite, it may play tricks on her. Expect your loved one to ask for certain dishes and then be unable to eat them. This can irritate everyone. Patients feel frustrated, and caregivers feel disappointed, or even resentful.

Stay awake to any need you might have to push food on your patient. These feelings say it's time to step back from caregiving and give care to yourself through gentle self-inquiry.

Looking deeply into neediness around food, we often find fear. Death scares us, and when we are afraid we get tight. Relax, take a breath, and fear not. Everything is in transition, but it's also at rest. Nature continually remakes itself while preserving its original state. We come from somewhere and we go somewhere but we remain completely at home. Relax, and breathe, breathe, breathe.

Our loved ones' dying is outside our control, but we can control how we respond to it. Knowing they might reject the food we prepare, we can make our shopping and cooking an offering. A few words of prayer or a simple chant said over a meal we prepare make it a ritual expression of our respect for life and our gratitude for the chance to serve.

Working in this spirit prepares us to accept rejection. When our patients can't eat what we cook, we don't feel threatened. We just scrape the untouched meal into the garbage with a shrug. Who knows? That uneaten eggplant Parmesan might be recycled as a rose.

HOME CARE NUTRITION

Nutrition is the science of studying how a living organism uses food. Dietitians draw on nutritional research to identify combinations of foods that help people recover from illness. These specialized diets strengthen the body's resistance to disease. We think of nutrition as eating to stay well or get healthy.

In the home care context, nutrition has a somewhat different definition. Dying people are giving up the body, not strengthening it. Their best diet is one that maintains the body through its gradual decline while providing as much eating pleasure as possible. In hospice, nutrition is primarily a quality of life issue.

This can be a source of confusion for caregivers. Don't try to make your patient conform to the usual rules of good nutrition. Cater to the food he craves and is able to eat.

Individuals vary greatly, but the home care standard is a high-calorie, high-protein diet based on the protein, dairy, and fat groups of foods. Throw out the weight-loss diet and bring on the ice cream! By the standards of hospice, ice cream is a wonderful multivitamin and high-calorie food. (Making it at home can be fun for you and your patient if you can find the time.)

A high-calorie, high-protein diet helps maintain weight and preserve proper chemical and fluid balances, but dying makes eating so problematic that this regimen is not always possible. When it isn't, the priority should be to help your loved one maintain calorie consumption and liquid intake for as long as possible. Offer plenty of between-meal snacks to keep up calorie consumption.

The best food for dying people is what tastes good—or at least can be tolerated—and leaves them feeling nourished. If I were dying I'd probably prefer pasta, whole grains, beans, fresh fruits, and vegetables because that's been my diet for years. Not everyone would agree. I recall with a shudder a patient who loved—gasp—pickled pigs' feet!

That adage from the sixties, "you are what you eat" definitely doesn't apply to the dying. Anything a dying person can eat and retain is good and helpful.

Allow your patient as much control as possible over the food she eats. Involve her in menu planning; making choices stimulates appetite. Ask her what she wants, listen well to what she requests, and observe her response to what's actually served.

Note how medications and medical treatments affect your patient's appetite. Record your observations in the Patient Log. (See the Home Skills section at the end of the chapter.)

If your patient is likely to be bedridden for months, you might want to check with an expert to make sure he gets the best possible balance of calories, proteins, vitamins, and minerals. Malnutrition can cause dehydration, skin breakdown, constipation, and other problems.

Unfortunately there is a lot of conflicting dietary information, and very little of it addresses the special needs of the dying. Your best bet is a registered dietitian (R.D.) with hospice experience. Ask the caregiving team doctor for a referral or look in the Yellow Pages under Health Care Services, Dietitians, and Nutritionists. You can also call the referral network at the American Dietetic Association, 800-877-1600.

The visiting nurse should be able to advise about diets that counteract diarrhea, constipation, and nausea.

TASTE TIPS

Dying people tend to prefer bland, familiar foods served in the usual plates and dishes. Don't be insulted if your loved one turns away from your fancy cooking and highly seasoned food. Plain cooking is best; boiling, steaming, baking, and broiling are better than frying. Instead of tart, spicy, and acidic seasonings, try using mild but distinctive seasonings such as lemon juice, basil, mint, and the patient's particular favorites. Keep serving temperatures tepid— cool down hot dishes and warm up cold ones.

Childhood favorites like macaroni and cheese may show up on your patient's wish list. On the other hand, she may get an occasional craving for something titillating. I've served up more than one slice of pepperoni pizza at the bedside.

Don't be afraid to experiment; sometimes a little creativity can arouse taste buds made dormant by medication and treatments. Check with the home meal service organizations in your area for tasty nonchew, high-protein, and high-calorie recipes. (AIDS agencies can be an excellent source of dietary information for anyone with a touchy appetite, not just people with HIV.)

Terminally ill people often have sore or infected mouths and throats that make chewing and swallowing painful. A little extra cutting, chopping, steaming, or mashing in the kitchen will make food more manageable while still preserving the distinct textures and flavors that give a dish interest.

Blenders make almost anything manageable, but entire blender meals reduce the quality of life. Don't puree solid foods until the person reaches the point where she can only consume liquids. When that time comes, you might want to consult the pureed foods cookbook created by Connecticut Hospice. For preparing tasty solid foods that can be easily swallowed, *The Non-Chew Cookbook* is a good source of ideas and inspiration. See Appendix 1: Resources for how to order either book.

Foods high in fat are harder to digest; don't serve them during periods of nausea or vomiting. If your patient has a problem with fatty foods, you can keep up the calories with foods high in protein and carbohydrates but low in fat. Try pudding with low-fat milk, low-fat yogurt and cheese, and juices.

If fat is not a problem, peanut butter is a great high-calorie food and flavor enhancer with a long shelf life. You can stir peanut butter into pudding right after cooking, add it to fruit smoothies, or roll it out in "Chews." Here's the recipe:

1 cup peanut butter
1 cup dry milk
½ cup raisins
¼ cup molasses

For the many patients who can't chew, two tablespoons of peanut butter stirred into a cup of yogurt makes a comforting, high-energy snack.

LOTS OF LIQUIDS

Terminally ill people require substantially less liquid, but they tend to drink even less than they need. Swallowing may be difficult. They may lack the energy and mental clarity to ask for the liquid they need. The body's decline may dull their sensitivity to thirst and make them unaware that drinking or sucking would make them feel better.

Dehydration can be a problem. Offer liquids often and make them easily accessible from the bed. Use non-spill cups, and keep flexible straws handy. If liquids are hard to swallow, squirt them into the mouth using a hypodermic syringe with the needle removed.

Freshly made fruit and vegetable juices are nourishing and tempting, but if your loved one prefers soda pop, honor this preference. Carbonated beverages may go down more easily if they're left to stand and lose some of their bubbles.

Popsicles are good. Any liquid can be frozen on a stick or made into ice chips for sucking. You might try to stimulate the patient's thirst by giving her salty broths or canned soups.

As death approaches, dehydration is a natural part of the process. Let nature take its course. If your loved one stops drinking entirely, keep his mouth moist with a swab and lubricate his lips with lip balm for comfort, but don't be compulsive about it. Providing food or drink intravenously or through tubes is an intervention not normally done in a hospice.

A less common problem arises when fluid intake is too high. Overhydration can cause fluid to accumulate in the tissues (edema), swell hands and feet, and even fill the lungs.

BLENDER DRINKS

The blender is an invaluable tool for whipping up nutritious fruit "smoothies" and milk shakes and mixing calorie and protein supplements like milk powder into sauces, soups, and juices.

For smoothies, keep a few bananas in the freezer (yes, bananas can be frozen) along with cans of orange juice concentrate to use as a base. Blend in ice cream, sherbet, honey, wheat germ, brewer's yeast, milk or milk powder, soy milk, nondairy creamer, yogurt, oat bran, cooked rice or commercial rice cakes, fresh or frozen fruit, applesauce, Carnation Instant Breakfast, Rice Dream, tofu, molasses—

you name it. (Avoid raw eggs because of the risk of salmonella.) The only limits are your imagination and your patient's tastes and diet intolerances.

Homemade blender drinks brimming with calories and proteins are superior to commercial nutrition beverages such as Ensure, Nutra Start, ReSource Plus, Sustacal, and Advera. These liquid "meals in a can" have many disadvantages. They are expensive, come in only a few flavors, have limited vitamins and minerals, contain little or no fiber, and don't appeal to unstable appetites because they aren't real food.

On the other hand, the caregiver can buy and store canned supplements for use when time is short, as it often is. This is a big plus. Also, the lack of fiber in commercial supplements can be an advantage in the last days, when the person stops consuming enough fluid to move fiber through the bowels. Chilling these beverages will make them more palatable. Adding ice cream also helps.

Many people are lactose intolerant and can't consume ice cream or other milk products. HIV tends to promote lactose intolerance.

EASY TO EAT

Offer meals in small amounts five or six times a day. Large servings intimidate frail appetites. Small, frequent meals optimize caloric intake while easing digestion by not overloading the stomach.

Sit down and eat some of the same food your loved one eats. Most people would prefer company at mealtimes. Keep conversation light and the atmosphere relaxed. Avoid talking about the quantity of food she eats, especially if you have to take a lot of it back uneaten.

Keeping to a regular eating schedule will help cue your loved one's body for sleep, but don't get too insistent. Encourage him to snack whenever and on whatever he likes. If you sense your patient might prefer solitude, let her eat alone for that meal. If she doesn't want to eat at all, sit with her during the usual times designated for meals to provide company and maintain a routine.

You also need regular, attractive, tasty meals eaten in the companionship of friends. Take good care of the caregiver. Schedule someone to relieve you occasionally so you can eat out.

Although you should never pressure your patient to eat, the following are ways to encourage appetite:

✦ A visually attractive meal tastes better. Decorate the food tray with a colored napkin or straw, a fresh-cut flower (if the scent isn't too strong), a paper doily, or a piece of origami. Coordinating the colors of foods with the colors of plates is a nice touch. Any simple thing that brings visual harmony to the meal will increase its pleasure.

✦ Exercise is an appetite stimulant provided that the workout isn't exhausting. Going for a walk, doing isometrics, or even receiving range-of-motion exercises while lying in bed will make food more appealing.

✦ A cocktail or a glass of white wine or sherry can open the taste buds, and the ceremony of bringing a drink to the bed signals the stomach that mealtime has arrived. Of course alcohol must not conflict with other medication. (Alcohol *is* a drug.)

✦ A change of environment can put someone in the mood for a meal. Eating in another room, or just getting out of bed and sitting in a chair, will help. Picnics in the park or in the backyard are great as long as the person's mobility is up to it.

✦ If your loved one can't change the environment, at least it can be altered. Create a mealtime atmosphere in the bedroom with background music, flowers, a change in lighting, candles.

✦ Marijuana—smoked, cooked in food, or taken as Marinol (dronabinol), a prescription drug—can stimulate appetite. So can other drugs like megestrol and dexamethasone, but marijuana has the bonus of effectively reducing nausea.

Nausea discourages eating and may produce vomiting. Nausea is caused by the disease process, by medical treatments, and by the anxiety common among hospice patients. Keep saltines handy for the first sign of nervous stomach. Ginger ale sometimes helps. Use plastic utensils to avoid adding a metallic taste to food.

Maintain good room ventilation to prevent noxious odors. Eliminate cigarette smoke. Keep the kitchen door closed while cooking to prevent food smells from traveling.

During periods of nausea, serve bland, low-fat foods like toast and soft-boiled eggs, and let your loved one sip liquids slowly through a straw. When nausea is acute, serve cold foods, which contain the fewest odors. After meals, keep the patient's head elevated to prevent vomiting.

If medications make the person nauseous, try not to medicate right before serving food. Medications and illness can cause hiccups and belching. To stop hiccups, give two teaspoons of sugar and have your loved one breathe into a paper bag. Or use any favorite family remedy. (Mine is drinking a glass of water through a washcloth!) Belching can be controlled by keeping the mouth closed when chewing or swallowing and by drinking liquids between, rather than during, meals.

Heartburn can be eased by wearing loose clothes, keeping the head elevated after meals, and eating frequent small snacks. Antacid in liquid form is the easiest to manage. Chill it to hide the chalky taste, and give it an hour before meals and at bedtime.

MOUTH CARE

Cleaning and caring for teeth and mouth make eating easier. Have your loved one brush his teeth and rinse out his mouth before meals. Use mouthwash or a mild saline solution unless the mouth is ulcerated or there are fissures of the tongue or bleeding gums. When this happens, use a swab and cold water to very carefully clean the mouth.

Because patients with advanced disease tend to lose weight, their gums may also shrink, and dentures may no longer fit well. Dentures that cause discomfort should be removed for eating and replaced afterward to preserve self-image. Treat dry or blistered lips with petroleum jelly.

Dry mouth is a common irritation for hospice patients. It is caused by dehydration, medications (opioids, antihistamines, antidepressants, and diuretics), oral infections like candidiasis ("thrush"—frequent among people with advanced disease), and tumors.

Moisten the mouth by offering sips of beverages, Popsicles, cracked ice, and hard candy to suck on. Keep an atomizer by the bed and spray often into the mouth. A vaporizer will add moisture to dry air.

When the mouth is dry, soups, casseroles, and custards are the easiest foods to eat. Fresh pineapple contains bromelain, an enzyme that cleans the mouth, but the canned fruit is easier to digest than the fresh. Chill and serve in chunks.

SERVING THE MEAL

Helping the patient eat is a major part of caregiving. The caregiver's day is often hurried, and eating is a slow process for a sick person. Try to budget enough time to cook and serve the meal without feeling rushed. Something very special is present in the moment when you and your patient bend to the task of keeping life going spoonful by spoonful.

Express your gratitude for this experience through mindful attention to the caregiver's craft. Approach your loved one in a spirit of listen and accept. Calm your mind and be fully present. As you greet the person, be alert to her eyes and gestures. Is she confused? Alert? Emotional? Neutral? With every movement and gesture speak your willingness to start right where she is.

Before bringing in the food, help her get set up for eating. Whenever possible, the patient should get out of bed and eat sitting in a chair. When not possible, help her get elevated in bed. Raise the head of the bed or prop up the patient with pillows. Then go get the food tray.

When you sit down with her, surrender completely to the situation. Feeding a patient is an utterly mutual experience. At mealtimes, we provide the food and our patients provide the chance for us to express our love for them. Relax and soften your belly. Breathe.

Honor the patient's need to preserve a sense of independence. Be unobtrusive. Let her salt, slice, butter, organize, and eat her food on her own; help only if necessary. If she has difficulty using a spoon or a fork, you might place the food on the utensil, help her grasp it, and then guide her hand to the mouth. Eating with the fingers is fine; wipe her hands with a napkin as needed.

When the mouth is tender, soften foods by dipping them in beverages, soups, and sauces. If he becomes easily confused, gently bring his attention back to his food by putting his hand to it. If his eyesight is impaired, talk to him through the meal. Describe each food and explain step by step what you are doing to help as you do it.

If the person wants to be fed and you think she can probably feed herself, she may be asking for attention. Provide it in more appropriate ways, such as reading to her.

At some point your loved one will need to be fed by hand. Here are the steps:

✦ Encourage him to sit up in bed to eat. If this isn't possible, put his head on a pillow.

✦ Make sure he can swallow.

✦ Be careful not to serve foods that are too hot; test the temperature first by putting a drop or two against your inner wrist.

✦ Cut solids into small amounts to avoid choking.

✦ When serving, you may have to cue him to open his mouth by touching the fork or spoon to his lower lip.

✦ Spoons should be filled only two-thirds full. Scrape off any drops from the bottom, lift the spoon to the patient's lower lip, and gently tilt the liquid into his mouth.

✦ Let him have plenty of time to swallow each bite before presenting the next one.

Keep the mouth moistened during the meal by having the person take a drink between bites. Drinks may be taken through a straw if the person can suck, but be sure to keep the lower end submerged so she doesn't suck up air. When offering liquids in a cup, support her head by putting your arm behind the pillow on which the head is resting. In the latter days liquids can be offered in a hypodermic syringe from which the needle has been removed. If your loved one isn't conscious, use a sponge swab instead. The syringe method can cause an unconscious person to choke.

ELIMINATION

We think of nutrition as solely concerned with the intake of food, but nutrition is a science that studies the entire relationship of food to the organism, including the elimination of waste. In thinking about keeping your patient well fed, you should think also about keeping her bowels working well. It's said Dr. Cicely Saunders, the founder of the modern hospice movement, delivered a lecture and slide show in which every fourth slide read, "Nothing matters more than the bowels!"[1]

Dying damages the body's capacity to process and control waste. People become incontinent or constipated or have frequent bouts of diarrhea. (Ninety percent of people with HIV disease experience diarrhea.)

Losing control of bladder and bowels is a hardship and a humiliation. Even a man as accustomed to difficulty as the poet Ryokan complained:

> Putting it in words
> it sounds
> so simple
> but with these runny bowels
> my body is hard to bear![2]

CLEAN AND DRY

If caregivers had a flag, the motto emblazoned on it would be "Clean and Dry." This is our call to action in the face of arduous circumstances. Keeping patients comfortable through their constant cycles of toilet care takes all the stamina and craft we can muster.

Toilet care taxes both us and our patients in emotional and physical ways. It roils the emotions by making caregiver and patient feel vulnerable. And it demands physical strength to get to the bathroom or the commode on time, lift up to use a bedpan, change diapers, strip a soiled bed and wash the sheets, and so on.

Toilet care is such hard work that we should encourage our patients to do it for themselves as long as they are able. This helps us, and it helps them, too. Sitting up, getting out of bed, and walking to the bathroom promotes more normal bowel movement and encourages a sense of independence. Eventually the dying person becomes too weak to get to the bathroom either on her own or with our help; then it's time to set up an alternative in the bedroom.

This may be a difficult moment. A loved one may find it hard to exchange the privacy of the bathroom for a toilet beside the bed, visible to everyone. He may see this as a public surrender of independence. You can ease the transition by explaining that a bedroom commode will save the embarrassment of not getting to the bathroom in time. When this is understood, the commode becomes a welcome resource rather than a threat. (One way to make it less threatening is to install the commode in the room from the start.)

Another big change takes place when the person loses control over bladder or bowels. This can be an upsetting, and even frightening, experience. Incontinence is undeniable evidence of the body releasing its functions on the path of letting go. We calm our loved ones' fear when we reassure them through word and gesture that cleaning up their "accidents" is perfectly OK with us.

STAGES OF TOILET CARE

Dying never follows a fixed route, but in planning for a patient's toilet care needs it's helpful to think of stages.

First Stage.

The patient gets out of bed and uses the toilet in the bathroom. (See Chapter 4 for tips on getting in and out of bed.) At this point the struggle is to maintain mobility. The person may use a cane or a walker; lean on the caregiver's arm; or go hand over hand following grab rails, a ballet barre, or even the backs of chairs lined up in a row.

If feeling weak, he may want to travel in a wheelchair or in an improvised rolling chair made from a regular chair with wheels or casters attached to the legs. If he becomes too weak to clean himself after defecation, he can be helped to his feet and then cleaned with toilet paper. During cleaning he can hold on to a grab bar or a towel rack for support.

Although the person is using the toilet during this stage, keep a plastic urinal, designed for either a male or a female, at the bed for convenience.

Second Stage.

A portable toilet is set up for use in the bedroom. This can be a specially made commode chair you rent or purchase from a hospital supply house, or you can use a sturdy wooden armchair and put a bedpan on it as needed. (Bedpans come in a variety of styles; consult with the hospice nurse.) A commode chair has the advantages of being lightweight, stable, easy to use and to clean, and reasonably comfortable. A regular chair is less conspicuous and saves space by doubling as a place to sit.

During this stage the patient weakens to the point where she can barely manage to get out of bed. The caregiver must move the patient from the bed to the toilet, using the steps described in Chapter 4.

Briefly, they are these:

✦ Place the portable toilet next to the bed. If it's a hospital bed, drop the side rail and lower the mattress to make it level with the toilet seat. If it's a regular bed, permanently adjust the mattress to the height of the toilet seat.

✦ Next, have your loved one move close to your edge of the bed and sit up if she can. Then, with your help if necessary, she swings her legs around and rests her feet on the floor.

a. If your loved one can't sit up, pull her to you using the draw-sheet and roll her onto her side, facing you. Slide her legs partially over the edge of the bed.

b. Then reach around and hold her across the shoulders with one arm, extending your hand upward to hold the neck. With the other hand, gently pull her toward you and into an upright position.

c. Continue the movement by using that hand to swing her legs around so her feet are touching the floor and she is sitting on the edge of the bed. (If her feet don't reach, you can lower the hospital bed.)

✦ Take a breath and get your balance. Then reach under your patient's armpits with both hands and hold her back at the shoulder blades.

✦ Finally, lean back, raise her from the edge of the bed, and pivot around to lower her onto the toilet.

Third Stage.

Getting out of bed has become so exhausting the person prefers to use a bedpan for defecation. The patient does this by lying on the back, bending the knees, bringing the heels as close as possible to the buttocks, and raising the hips while the caregiver slides the bedpan under. If the patient lacks the strength to raise up, the caregiver can place one hand under the lower back and lift while sliding the bedpan under with the other hand.

By this time the person may have lost control of his bladder. Urinary incontinence can be managed by having the hospice nurse insert a tube, or catheter, through the urethra into the bladder, where a tiny inflated balloon holds it in place. The other end of this Foley catheter is attached to a collection bag.

The system is simple, but some people feel encumbered or irritated by the tubing, and a confused patient may try to pull it out. Men have the option of using a condom catheter, which is attached externally to the penis and has less chance of causing irritation.

The catheter system can be made completely portable, and it permits monitoring the patient's urinary output and quality. Always empty the collection bag before it becomes so full that urine backs up in the catheter and carries infectious bacteria into the person's urinary tract. Before turning a patient to prevent bedsores or change the sheets, drain the bag and put it on the side of the bed toward which you are turning the patient.

Fourth Stage.

The person has lost control of both bowels and bladder, is very weak and often quite thin, and must depend entirely on the caregiver for managing elimination. At this point there are many options. The best one reflects both your loved one's preferences and your need to conserve time and money.

A Foley or a condom catheter will channel urine to a collection bag, but the small amount of fluid produced at this stage may not merit the possible discomfort. A disposable adult diaper can contain both urine and stool, but the thought of wearing a diaper makes some people uncomfortable. Another option is a disposable underpad like Chux or Curity that can be thrown away after each use. The underpad can be laid on a plastic pad to save the bottom sheet. (Never place plastic directly under a person because it will retain moisture and damage the skin.) Some people lay several sheets of newspaper on top of the bottom sheet and then cover the newspaper with a drawsheet, which can be laundered.

Note that even when a person has stopped eating entirely and is very close to death the body continues to burn stored protein and eliminate waste.

TOILET CARE TIPS

✦ If the person might need help while using the commode, a stand-alone screen will provide some privacy while the caregiver remains in the room. An alternative is to leave and wait to be called back.

✦ Ventilate the room immediately after the bedside toilet is used; lingering odors discourage visitors.

✦ The person may get easily chilled while using the toilet or bedpan. Cover her with a sheet, a shawl, or a blanket. This is also a way to afford some privacy if the patient needs to be held up to use the commode.

✦ Bedpans come in two basic types. The "fracture pan" is flatter and easier to place under the buttocks. Plastic bedpans are better than metal ones because they don't get so cold to the touch.

✦ Always ask your patient if he wants to use the commode or the bedpan before, not after, changing the sheets.

✦ A diaper may not fully contain diarrhea. You might want to use a Chux or Curity underpad as well.

✦ The seat on the toilet in the bathroom can be raised to make it easier for the person to sit down and stand up.

✦ Sometimes parents won't allow opposite-sex children to help with toilet care. Acceptance may be easier if a nurse or doctor requests their cooperation as a "medical necessity."

✦ When flushing stool down the toilet, note its consistency and color and record any significant changes in the Patient Log (see the Home Skill section at the end of the chapter.)

In conclusion, remember that dying doesn't follow fixed stages. Any particular toilet need may show up at any point in the process. For example, a person who usually uses the toilet in the bathroom may want to keep a bedpan handy for emergencies.

CLEANING WITH COMPASSION

Cleaning our loved ones after a bowel movement may seem at first like a forbidding task, but we quickly find we want to do it well because they need our help so much. It's a vital job. Urine and excrement can damage fragile skin and cause painful, hard-to-heal bedsores. To prevent irritation and infection, we should clean our patients as gently and as thoroughly as we ourselves would like to be cleaned. If the smell makes you feel nauseous, try putting a little Vicks VapoRub under your nose.

Put on latex gloves. Wipe the area with soft toilet paper or tissues. Then use disposable wipes or a washcloth and warm, soapy water to clean carefully, paying attention to the folds of the buttocks. Dry the area completely. Apply a lanolin lotion or a barrier cream to protect the skin.

When managing and disposing of body substances such as feces, urine, and blood, observe the Universal Infection Precautions as adapted to a home health care setting. Your hospice should be able to provide you with these generally accepted guidelines.

CONSTIPATION

Constipation is common among the terminally ill. Lack of exercise; poor appetite; a diet low in fiber; dehydration due to a low intake of liquids, diarrhea, or vomiting; and opioid narcotics and other medications—all tend to clog "the plumbing." Difficulty in getting out of bed may further discourage elimination by making it seem too much trouble to get up and go to the bathroom.

Constipation can be a serious medical condition. It weakens the body by cutting off nutrients; causes intense discomfort that can make the person tense, restless, and fearful; and can lead to complications such as bowel obstructions and hemorrhoids.

Prevention is easier than cure. Using the toilet should be made as easy as possible. Any requests your loved one might express—a heater in the bathroom, more privacy in the bedroom—should be honored if possible.

Any patient taking an opioid painkiller like morphine should automatically receive at the same time a regular laxative dose. Keep food fiber at the highest level that the person's taste, digestive system, and intake of liquids can comfortably accommodate. Physical activities such as sitting up, getting out of bed, walking, and doing isometrics and range-of-motion exercises encourage digestion. Abdominal massage also helps.

On the other hand, the body shuts down in the process of dying, and this leads to fewer bowel movements. The elimination habits of a lifetime must be given up along with life itself.

Irregularity can be very upsetting, especially to an older loved one. The hospice nurse will probably not suggest laxatives unless his bowels haven't moved for three days or he feels discomfort. In the meantime you can reassure him by establishing and explaining a clear policy for how you will help when necessary. For example: "If there is no bowel movement in x hours, I will give you some milk of magnesia."

Nearly all hospice patients eventually require a regular laxative. Start by using whatever has worked for the person in the past. Gentle natural laxatives and herbal teas are best; bulk-forming laxatives like Metamucil can cause impaction if the person isn't drinking the usual amount of liquid. Sometimes all that's needed is a stool-softening agent.

If constipation persists, the hospice doctor or nurse will suggest increasingly potent laxatives until results are obtained. (Like painkillers, laxatives climb a ladder of potency.) When constipation is severe, disposable enemas that are safe and easy to use can be purchased over the counter. Rectal suppositories produce fast relief when discomfort is acute. If there is evidence of oozing stool, call the nurse.

DIARRHEA

A dying person's delicate stomach, the disease process, overuse of laxatives, drug and treatment side effects, and constipation (oozing stool) can cause diarrhea. Diarrhea is especially common among people with AIDS. Provide a high-liquid, low-fiber diet of bland foods plus doses of Pepto-Bismol or Kaopectate. Metamucil is effective for treating alternating diarrhea and constipation. Be sure to keep the skin in the affected area clean and dry and apply a protective ointment. Clean and dry!

Home Skill: Setting Up the Patient Log

Keeping a daily bedside log is vital to the well-being of the patient. The log tracks details about medications, meals, toilet use, doctor's appointments, and care problems. It serves as a health care record, a reminder to caregivers, and an essential resource enabling visiting nurses and doctors to accurately assess the patient's condition in order to prescribe appropriate medicines and therapies.

The log is particularly important for evaluating pain medications. Carefully record the amount and time of each dose and note the effect. Does the medication relieve pain? Induce sleep? Cause anxiety? As Andrea Sankar notes in *Dying at Home,* "If the physician or nurse fails to relieve the pain and makes no use of the Patient Log, consider switching to a different doctor or nurse."[3]

Jot down what food was served and how it was received. Keep track of toilet use, and when flushing stool down the toilet, observe its consistency and color and make a note in the log. Also note when the bedridden patient is turned to prevent bedsores.

If the patient can help keep the log, this will give some feeling of control, but the important thing is to maintain the continuity of information so members of the caregiving team can read the log and be quickly brought up to date. As the pressures of caregiving mount, important details will be forgotten if they aren't written down. After death, the log provides a record of the patient's last days for family and friends.

The log can be of any format as long as it divides the day into quickly referenced time segments and provides space for entries in four areas: medication, meals, elimination, and turning to prevent bedsores. Doctor's appointments and general comments can be written underneath the daily schedule. Caregivers can write their more personal observations and experiences on the back of the page.

Your nurse may have a ready-made form, or you may want to design your own using the following example. Lay out the log template on a piece of typewriter paper. (Two patient days per page works well.) Then have it photocopied and hole-punched for a three-ring binder, which is kept by the bedside. The patient's weekly pill schedule can be taped to the back of the Mediset box in which the pills are kept.

Date:	*Reminder:*			
	Medicine/dosage/time taken	Meals	Toilet	Turn
4:00A.M.–7:00A.M.				
7:00A.M.–10:00A.M.				
10:00A.M.–1:00P.M.				
1:00P.M.–4:00P.M.				
4:00P.M.–7:00P.M.				
7:00P.M.–10:00P.M.				
10:00P.M.–1:00A.M.				
1:00A.M.–4:00A.M.				
Comments:				

Eight

Easing Pain and
Learning Its Lessons

True religion is surrender.
—Mohammed

P AIN IS A STUBBORN PART OF LIFE'S PROCESS, but resistance only
makes it worse. This was the great teaching of the natural childbirth movement. Mothers learned that when they didn't make pain
an enemy, they suffered less during delivery. Instead they made
peace with pain by accepting it on its own difficult terms.

On the other hand, pain is not desirable. As caregivers we should
encourage our loved ones to approach their dying with an attitude
of "no heroics." We should seek complete pain control through medication and other therapies.

Complete control is the goal but not the reality. At present we
can't guarantee that our loved ones will have pain-free dying. We
can only promise that any pain which can't be eliminated will be
compassionately shared.

I was reminded of that one Friday afternoon. Tired by a week of
work, I pulled into the hospice parking lot looking forward to renewal with my friends. No sooner had I entered the ward than a
nurse's aide rushed up and asked me to help her with a new patient.
She said we had to lift him from his bed and lay him on a gurney
so he could be wheeled off and given a bath. I wrote down in my
journal what happened next.

As we drew near to his bed the stench was so great that neither of us could do anything until I opened a window. At first I thought the smell was excrement, but then she pulled back the sheet to reveal the gangrenous flesh around the dark red valley of the hip socket. A wound had rotted out his pelvis like a tree stump.

I turned away to look at the young man's face. Pain contorted his handsome features. As we began to lift him he gripped the underside of his ruined thigh in anguish, protesting in an Asian language. We tried to be gentle, but he fought us all the way. At last we got him on the gurney, and with a little stroking managed to persuade him to lie back enough to be wheeled away.

Then for the first time I noticed the young pair watching from the foot of the bed. She stood riveted to the spot as if in shock while he twisted like a leaf in the wind. The pain in their hearts was completely transparent.

When I approached them, she explained in accented English that she was the patient's girlfriend, and her companion was his brother. She said they worried that he wouldn't get his painkillers. His name—Nguyen—and their features suggested that they were ethnic Chinese from Vietnam, so I thought it would reassure them to talk with the head nurse, who is also Chinese. It did. The three of them had a long conversation, and although I couldn't understand what they said, I could see its positive impact. The girlfriend, especially, seemed greatly relieved, and afterward she thanked me profusely.

By this time Nguyen had been bathed and returned to his curtained-off bed, so I left the three of them together. Later I saw Dr. Kerr arrive to cut away the gangrenous flesh, but I was busy with other patients and then the afternoon was over.

When I left, Nguyen's bed was still curtained off. By the time I returned the next week he had died. And that's it. I learned no more of his story. I suspect he had been in a refugee camp, where his wound had been grossly neglected, but that's only a guess. All I know for certain is that Nguyen died deeply loved by two compassionate people.

Nguyen's circumstances were extreme. People dying at home don't usually go through such hell. But that doesn't mean they don't hurt. Dying often brings with it moments of deep physical and emotional anguish.

Pain relief is the heart of home care. The caregiver can always find creative and helpful ways to respond to a dying person in pain, using all available tools.

In responding to physical pain, medication is the principal resource. In the past there was a lot of talk about helping people die with minds unclouded by drugs. Practice, however, taught that terminal illness can cause pain so intense that it clouds the mind on its own.

Perhaps two-thirds of terminal patients require pain medication at some point in their dying. The dosage, not the drugs, is the issue. At what point does the pain medication dull awareness and at what point does the pain itself do this? Look for the right balance between pain control and mental clarity.

Ultimately our patients know best. As conscious caregivers we accept what our loved ones tell us about their pain, and we accept their right to meet it in the way they want. Acceptance itself is a pain reliever because it communicates trust and bridges the isolation that is dying's worst pain.

WHAT IS PAIN?

Chronic pain is so common in America today that pain control has become a multibillion-dollar industry spawning highly sophisticated experts, but it all comes down to one person. Pain is utterly personal. The dictionary defines it as "an unpleasant sensation," but what is unpleasant for me might not be so for you. Each of us defines for ourselves what constitutes pain.

Pain lacks an absolute standard. Hospice patients are asked to rank their pain from 1 to 10 as a way of determining what they find tolerable, but that doesn't mean one person's 5 equals another's. Each scale is unique to each individual. Scientists can calculate the size of the earth and the speed of light, but no one has ever devised a way to quantify pain.

The intensity, quality, and frequency of pain, as well the meaning given to it, are subjective. This has important practical and spiritual implications. The spiritual implication is that we must investigate on our own the meaning of our pain and what it teaches us. The practical implication is that a dying person's pain-relief regimen can't be standardized.

Caregivers and patients must together work out an individualized plan for pain control that establishes the remedies and medications needed. The plan requires frequent review because the patient's condition is always changing. The Patient Log (see the Home Skill section at the end of Chapter 7) plays an important part in the review process. Listen closely to what your patient tells you about her pain.

Some people find pain very hard to describe. The American Cancer Society and the National Cancer Institute suggest asking the following questions as a way of guiding people in pain toward an explanation of what they're feeling.

✦ Where do you feel your pain?

✦ When did it begin?

✦ How bad is it?

✦ Does it prevent you from doing your daily activities? Which ones?

✦ What relieves your pain?

✦ What makes it worse?

✦ What have you tried for pain relief? What helped? What didn't?

✦ What have you done in the past to relieve other kinds of pain?

✦ Is the pain constant? If not, how many times a day (or week) does it occur?

✦ How long does it last each time?[1]

THE NEW MODEL OF PAIN RELIEF

In recent years medicine has developed a wide variety of **analgesic** (pain-reducing), antidepressant, anti-inflammatory, and muscle relaxant drugs to help terminal patients cope with their trying physical and mental symptoms. In large part this is an achievement of the hospice movement. By insisting that health professionals pay attention to symptom management, and not just disease prevention, the movement stimulated research in new drugs and new ways to administer them.

The old model of pain relief derived from crisis medicine. It provided short-term treatment for an acute condition resulting from bodily injury. Doctors and nurses concerned about addiction would administer narcotics only on an "as needed" basis, **P.R.N.** in medical jargon. Patients had to experience their pain before the drugs were delivered.

This approach is inadequate. Dying people are subject to chronic physical pain that can be terribly intense. Pain results from the disease, from therapies to treat the disease (chemotherapy, irradiation), and from bedridden inactivity.

When medication is given only after the onset of pain, doses must be very large. Large, infrequent doses tend to cloud the mind and produce nausea and other unpleasant side effects.

Moreover, the as-needed approach made chronic patients fearful. It trained them to expect pain, and the expectation of pain can be worse than the experience. Pioneers like Dr. Cicely Saunders discovered how to unlearn the expectation of pain by administering frequent, smaller amounts of medication.

Today we advise giving around-the-clock regular dosages before, rather than after, the pain strikes. This has a better chance of keeping patients in a steady, pain-free state and produces fewer unwanted effects. And by diminishing the worry that pain will suddenly return, regular pain management helps patients help themselves. Studies show that through the placebo effect patients who expect pain relief actually create their own biomedical pain relievers, called endorphins.

MANAGING PAIN THROUGH MEDICATION

There are analgesics, both prescription and nonprescription, for every type and level of discomfort. The hospice doctor should explain the options to the satisfaction of both you and your patient and make a recommendation based on the patient's particular physical and mental condition.

The doctor needs feedback to establish an effective pain management plan. You may have to try several combinations before the right mix of drugs and dosages is found. Keep track of your patient's responses in the Patient Log and inform the attending physician.

Managing medication is an important part of caregiving. To play your proper role, you'll need to know the following:

✦ The names of all medications, not just those used for pain relief

✦ What they are for

✦ How often they are taken

✦ Whether they should be taken with food or on an empty stomach

✦ Possible side effects

✦ How they interact with other drugs, including alcohol and caffeine, and with nutritional supplements

A tip: Pharmacists are highly trained experts. Make friends with your local druggist.

In talking about pain, it helps to have a common language. You may find the Levels of Pain table helpful.

Levels of Pain

	None	Mild	Moderate	Severe
Person is VERBAL	Ask person to rate or describe pain by using numbers or words.			
	Facial expression and body relaxed. Quiet, peaceful sleep. Participates in normal activity.	Restless, frequent movements seeking comfortable position. Intermittent sleep or normal activity patterns. Rubbing or touching the painful body part.	Difficulty concentrating or maintaining normal activity pattern. Difficulty sleeping, with periods of time awake at night. Guarding or immobilizing body part that hurts.	Impossible to maintain normal activity pattern or sleep at night. May moan or cry.
Person is NON-VERBAL	Gently touching suspected area of pain			
	Elicits no response.	Elicits withdrawal.	Elicits withdrawal or soft vocalization.	Elicits sharp withdrawal and loud vocalization.

Source: Laguna Honda Hospital

NARCOTICS

Pain tends to rise as dying approaches and then fall off completely in the very last hours. As the pain becomes more severe, stronger medications are needed to relieve it. The "analgesic ladder" rises from aspirin and the nonsteroidal anti-inflammatory agents (the so-called **NSAIDs**, such as ibuprofen) through the mild opiates like codeine to full-strength opiates such as morphine and methadone.

A doctor may prescribe both opiates and nonopiates to achieve the best pain control with the fewest side effects. The NSAIDS, for example, help relieve the dull, aching pain of bone cancer.

Not all terminal patients in pain require an opiate, but for those that do, **morphine** is the popular choice. Morphine is easy to take and enters the bloodstream quickly. Common brand names are Roxanol, a liquid, and MS Contin, a timed-release tablet.

The traditional analgesic meperidine (Demerol) is ineffective and has troublesome side effects, including the possibility of seizure. Meperidine has been in use so long that it has won wide acceptance, but well-informed health professionals no longer prescribe it.

Pain relievers are usually administered orally. Liquid morphine is typically given every four hours mixed with juice or any other water-based liquid. If the person is unable to handle a cup, morphine can be injected into the mouth through a syringe from which the hypodermic needle has been removed. Timed-release morphine tablets help a patient get through the night. A double dose of liquid morphine given at bedtime also works. Short-acting rectal suppositories provide quick relief for breakthrough pain.

When the patient can't take oral pain medication, the doctor may prescribe an adhesive **patch** containing the narcotic fentanyl (Duragesic). The patch lasts for two or three days. It is fixed to the upper arm or back and worn continually, even in the shower. Although convenient, fentanyl patches are expensive, can come loose with perspiration, and may take as long as twelve to forty-eight hours to reach full effect.

Pain management through medication is as much an art as a science. Some experts believe pain is so subjective and unpredictable that administering relief should be left up to the patient. This was the thinking behind the development of a book-sized **infusion pump** that releases narcotics directly into the bloodstream both automatically and on patient demand.

Because of their cost and relative complexity compared with a simple syringe, pain-control analgesia (PCA) pumps are now used mostly in hospitals. Studies have shown them to be effective, however, so they may be more common in home care in the future.

Pain medicines, especially the stronger ones, tend to have side effects. This should be anticipated. Morphine and all opiates will constipate and may induce some nausea and drowsiness. Constipation and nausea can be counteracted through medication, and the drowsiness will abate in a few days, when the person's body adjusts. Opiates can produce some degree of physical dependence, but this is not the same as addiction.

FEAR OF ADDICTION

Studies have shown that the most common form of narcotic abuse in terminal care is the undermedication of pain. Hospital physicians routinely underprescribe for dying patients because the medical establishment harbors an excessive concern about fostering addiction.[2]

Many patients share this fear. Laboring under the mistaken idea that "less is better" when it comes to narcotics, some consistently underreport their pain and take less medication than needed to maintain a steady, pain-free state. Others see themselves as becoming addicted as drug dosages start to increase with increasing pain. They refuse prescribed doses even when their pain reaches extraordinary levels.

It's very important for patients taking narcotics to understand that drug addiction is largely irrelevant in the hospice context. Yes, patients receiving opiates over time will develop a physical tolerance—a dependence, if you will. This can be easily handled by increasing the dose to maintain comfort. But patients won't become compulsive drug seekers unless they have a preexisting habit. When narcotics are used to treat physical, rather than emotional, needs, addiction is very rarely a problem.

We ease the pain of a loved one when we help her let go of false moral or medical judgments about drug addiction. Hospice exists to allow dying people to live their last weeks or days with as much clarity and comfort as possible. Narcotics can help this happen.

BALANCING PAIN AND AWARENESS

Using drugs to balance pain against awareness requires the dying person, the physician, the hospice nurse, and the primary caregiver to explore together the proper medication and dosage. Keep a record of what makes your loved one feel better and what doesn't help.

The last word belongs to the patient if at all possible. As the patient grows weaker and less able to articulate needs, the caregiver's day-to-day observations increase in importance.

The Pain Management Committee at San Francisco General Hospital sets the following goals for balancing pain medication against patient mental awareness:

✦ Prevent chronic pain.

✦ Erase the memory and expectation of pain with scheduled dosing.

✦ Allow the patient to remain alert and to function.

✦ Allow the patient to have and express feelings.

✦ Do all this with the greatest possible ease for the caregiver and the family.

When a person is comatose, he can still experience pain and need medication. Behaviors such as restlessness, wincing, groaning, and picking at the skin help the caregiver and doctor determine proper dosages.

You and your loved one's doctor will feel more ethically comfortable about making dosage decisions if the dying person has specified in advance her pain-relief preferences. Talk over the options while she is still cogent. Is her biggest fear pain? Or is she more concerned about being "snowed under" by drugs? Write out her instructions and have her sign this advance directive.

In cases of extreme pain the doctor may suggest a nerve block. Substances are injected into or around a nerve ending to block it from transmitting pain. This causes loss of all feeling in the affected area and may produce muscle paralysis. Nerve blocks are also used when the person experiences unacceptable side effects from general pain medicine.

During the period of active dying, friends and loved ones may suffer more than the person doing the dying. Resist the temptation to give medication to a comatose person to offset *your* pain. Take comfort from reports by near-death survivors who say that physical pain was not a part of their experience. Even when their bodies appeared to be racked with pain they were actually in a painless state.

NONDRUG THERAPIES

People vary widely in their experience of pain and in their response to the many methods of relieving it. Some find relief without using medicine. Others combine drugs and nondrug therapies. You and your patient should experiment. Keep a record of what works and what doesn't.

✦ Gentle *touch* relieves mild pain; a foot or hand massage reassures without putting pressure on sensitive mid-body areas.

✦ Applying *heat* to the painful area stimulates circulation and relieves sore muscles. The easiest and most convenient means are the heating pad, the hot pack, and the ever-faithful hot-water bottle wrapped in a towel to prevent burning. (Putting a second hot-water bottle against the feet sets up a helpful top-to-bottom circulatory pattern.) Bedridden people have fragile skin. Be careful not to turn the heating pad too high or leave it on all night.

✦ Some people prefer treatment with *cold* rather than heat (cryotherapy as opposed to thermotherapy). Cold diminishes pain sensations by numbing the affected area. Try an ice pack or ice cubes wrapped in a towel. Even better are the gel packs available at drugstores. Don't use a cold so intense or so lengthy that it itself causes pain. If your patient starts to shiver, remove the cold at once.

✦ Place a washcloth on the forehead; it can be either cool or warm, depending on the person's preference.

✦ Many topical pain-relieving *menthol preparations* such as Ben-

Gay and Heet are available over the counter. Spread on the skin, these preparations increase blood circulation to the treated area and produce a soothing feeling that lasts for several hours. Before using menthol extensively, be sure to test a small area of the skin and check for irritation.

✦ *Distraction* can relieve mild pain for hours and is effective against intense pain for short periods of time. Television is the most popular means, but anything that absorbs attention can be tried, such as reading to your loved one or engaging her in conversation.

✦ *Music* can be a very powerful antidote to pain. Keep handy favorite tapes and CDs. Slow, familiar rhythms are best. Listening through headphones concentrates the experience. If your patient finds music too demanding try "white noise," like an electric fan.

✦ With the help of special *biofeedback* machines, people can learn to control such body functions as heart rate, blood pressure, and muscle tension. Doing this gives them freedom from the awareness of their pain. Biofeedback is usually combined with other pain-relief methods.

✦ *Guided imagery* is an easy and effective relaxation technique you can do together. Ask what environments he finds relaxing. For example: lying on the bank of a river; sitting in a garden in spring; being on the beach listening to the ocean. Then have him close his eyes and in a soothing voice guide him through an imaginary experience of this setting. Check with your home care team for guided imagery audiotapes.

✦ *Acupuncture* and *hypnosis* relieve pain for some but not others. Anyone undergoing chemotherapy should receive acupuncture only under professional guidance.

✦ *TENS*, or transcutaneous electrical nerve stimulation, uses a small power pack to relieve pain by applying mild electric currents to areas of the skin.

✦ People with chronic pain sometimes find relief through *meditation*, but don't expect a patient who has never meditated to begin a new mental discipline at the end of her life.

The comeditation technique explained in the Home Skill section at the end of the chapter doesn't run this risk because the patient plays a passive rather than active role. Comeditation induces a profound relaxation that facilitates, rather than frustrates, dying.

BREATHING THROUGH THE PAIN

Breathing is one therapy that works with anyone, whether living or dying. When we see a loved one in pain, one of the first things we can do is calmly remind her to breathe.

Pain tends to block breathing. The person in pain tightens against it by contracting the diaphragm. This makes the pain worse in two ways. First, because the diaphragm is anchored to the ribs, tensing it stiffens the body and intensifies the feeling of pain. Second, when insufficient air reaches the lungs to oxygenate the blood, the person feels out of breath and even more anxious. He becomes vulnerable to a full-blown panic attack that may require drugs to resolve.

Relief is just a breath away. Breathing begins an immediate relaxation response. Have the person slowly inhale a breath and then exhale it into the painful area, allowing the breath to caress and care for the hurt.

Let him fill and release the lungs as best he can. Don't make him feel he has to accomplish anything special. Shortness of breath, or dyspnea, is common among dying people in pain and can't be willed away. (If dyspnea is chronic, the doctor may prescribe one of the opiate drugs to slow respiration.)

If he is having trouble breathing, change his position in bed and elevate his head 20 to 30 degrees. If he is wheezing or gasping, gently bring him to a sitting position and use pillows or towels to prop him up. Check for mucus accumulated in the mouth and throat. Remove the mucus with a swab if your loved one is too weak to care for himself. A humidifier will loosen secretions that tend to accumulate in the airway, especially if oxygen is in use. Oxygen has a drying effect.

When your loved one is experiencing a bad moment of pain, try to find time to remain at her bedside. When you see her chest and stomach stiffen, softly remind her to gently inhale and then exhale into the pain. At the same time, bring your attention completely into the present by focusing on your own breath. Focused breathing is mind expanding. It moves us from "my mind" to Big Mind, from talking about life to living it, from fear to acceptance.

FEAR INTENSIFIES PAIN

Fear and pain are similar self-defense responses; both stiffen and contract the body against the perception of threat. When present together, fear and pain amplify each other: when someone in pain is scared, the pain hurts more. Thus anything that relieves the fear will also relieve the pain.

More than anything, a dying person fears abandonment. As caregivers we can relieve this fear by promising to be there to the end. We make this vow convincing through the creative little ways we try to meet each fear as it arises. Our strong commitment finds practical expression. For example, if your loved one is afraid at night, you might sleep in the same room with her. To provide even more comfort, tie a string to your hand and give her the other end to hold for security.

Another profound fear in dying is loss of control. The future no longer is. The past comes back to haunt with regrets. The present totters on the edge of dementia and incontinence. Against this anxious background, pain looms as a constant presence. Will it strike again? Will it get worse?

Caregivers can restore calm by giving the dying person power to manage his pain through medication. Reassure your patient that his pain will always be addressed. Have him write out and sign an advance directive specifying the precise ways he can signal a need for pain medication in the event he is unable to speak.

Fear is contagious. Loved ones' pain can make their caregivers fearful. Seeing their dying we fear our own. Their death seems a personal threat. It isn't. Change is impersonal. Everything passes. Even fear.

Find the courage to stay present. Acknowledge your fear, set it aside, and return to attending your loved one in pain. As conscious caregivers we are aware of our own needs, but we always put the needs of our patients first. There is time later to reflect on our own fearful feelings.

PAIN AND SUFFERING

Although we talk about physical and emotional pain as if they were different, no real boundary exists. The mind and body are one.

Dr. Cicely Saunders says pain is "total." It results from the complex interactions of physical sensations and emotional states.[3] Dr. Robert Brody, San Francisco General Hospital's authority on pain, says much the same thing when he calls pain "a person's emotional experience of a distressing sensation."[4]

Everyone knows that the physical sensation of pain can stir up the emotions. Let's say I go to hammer a nail but instead I hit my finger. As a result, my finger hurts and I'm furious. The origin of the hurt is obvious, but where does the fury come from? The answer lies in understanding the difference between pain and suffering.

Pain can originate either in the mind or in the body. It starts in the body when tissue is damaged and the nerves transmit an emergency message. If I hit myself with a hammer, I experience a very clean, clear signal that something needs attention. This is pain.

The suffering kicks in because I don't like having a sore finger. Suffering is the "something extra" I add to a painful event. Suffering is dissatisfaction with the way things are.

How we interpret our pain, how much dissatisfaction we inject into it, depends on mood, morale, experiences, and the meaning we give to it. If my feet hurt because I'm running a race it may seem perfectly OK. (One of the contestants in the 1996 Boston Marathon ran with a sign saying, "Pain is brief, but pride is forever.") In this case the unpleasant sensation is likely to remain near the level of pure pain, and I may not suffer much at all. But if I stub my toe against a chair and then get mad at my clumsiness, I hurt even more. Should I get myself really worked up—let's say I remember other stubbed toes and conjure up my life as nothing but one long series of crippling blows to the foot—I can make a minor sensory experience into something excruciating.

Pain is what happens; suffering is our negative interpretation of it. Dying people often get caught in a cross fire of pain and suffering. The body's deterioration is not always the origin of the agony, as in this case, taken from my journal.

> Entering the men's ward I found Guo Fu Hung propped up in bed, smiling sweetly. Mr. Hung was often smiling. His colon cancer didn't cause him much pain.
>
> Mr. Hung came to hospice after owning a shop on a busy corner in Chinatown for forty years. The business let him and his now deceased wife raise a son and daughter. He showed me their photographs. He also showed me a photo of his tombstone and grave site in a San Francisco suburb. He said he made all the preparations for his death because he couldn't trust his children to do it.
>
> "The children here are not like in China." His smile failed him when he said this. His son and daughter didn't come to see him very often; his grandchildren came only once. Tears welled up in his eyes when he talked about them. Mr. Hung was not experiencing much pain, but he was suffering nonetheless.

All of us are experts in turning our pain into suffering. We train ourselves to do this. Life doesn't meet our expectations, so we make ourselves suffer. The ants at a picnic bother us because we think they are optional.

Pain is not an option in life, but we still try to escape it. In America this mad dash is raised to the level of a constitutional principle called the pursuit of happiness. It's just a rat race. Avoiding pain and chasing pleasure dooms us to endless frustration because pain is inherent in existence. The wise old husband of an elderly woman who died told me afterward, "When you wake up in the morning and you don't feel any pain, then you know you're dead."

Pain is a part of our human condition, but that doesn't mean it has to define who we are. We have a choice. Instead of running away, we can slow down long enough to see clearly what it is we've been avoiding. And we give it the healing attention it demands. Letting go of our resistance to pain, we let go of resistance to life, and we stop suffering.

THEIR PAIN, AND OURS

Charles Garfield, the founder of San Francisco's widely emulated Shanti Project, says caregivers with deep emotional wounds are better qualified to empathize with those facing life-threatening illness. But he cautions that "wounded healers" must acknowledge and accept their wounds before they can help heal others.[5]

As conscious caregivers we are aware of the difference between our pain and the pain of our dying loved ones. Although we attend to theirs first, we don't ignore our own. Getting tough with ourselves only hardens our hearts against everyone. Staying open to our pain makes us more sensitive to the pain of our patients.

Through empathy we are able to experience the pain of others as if it were ours. Through compassion we choose to do so. Compassion is the willingness to let our hearts be touched by pain and the heartfelt wish to end suffering by reaching out and touching others.

Compassion means "to suffer with," but this is not just a passive, warmhearted feeling. Compassion is sympathy in action. The Buddhist saint of compassion, Avalokiteshvara, is depicted with a thousand arms that enable him to extend support in every direction.

Compassionate action overcomes pain's alienation. Since pain is personal and cannot be transferred, it tends to isolate. The loneliness can be acute for dying people, whose pain can't be cured and will end only in death.

Loneliness is not always bad. Sometimes patients need to be left alone so they can feel their pain and heal it. There may be relationships to resolve within; there may be memories to reexperience. A compassionate response supports this process without smothering it.

When we touch and take care of our dying loved ones, when we listen with an open heart, we affirm in a very credible way their importance to us, and this lends their pain meaning. Experienced in the context of a meaningful life, pain is far more tolerable.

Each time we open our hearts to another's pain, we nurture our compassion. Compassion is the flower of our nature, and caregiving lets it bloom. But softening the heart to another's pain isn't easy. It takes plenty of courage, patience, and commitment. As caregivers we should honor our effort by not condemning ourselves when we feel we can't cope.

Even the worst moments of hopeless despair can be accepted if we remember that everything changes. The pain that seems so solid and concrete dissolves like a cloud when we give it our full attention, and let it pass. We let go of judging our caregiving and ourselves; we stop rejecting what was unacceptable. In denying nothing, we find that everything is ours. The unguarded heart knows that all beings are one, and we feel great joy. This is how compassion heals us. Surrendering to things as they are, we find universal support.

MEDITATION

Accepting ourselves, coming into harmony with our pain, we encourage acceptance and harmony in others. But acceptance is a quest; we don't get there all at once. When the journey gets long, meditation is a ready refuge.

Meditation softly contains our pain while we learn how to live with it. Through meditation we strengthen the heart's compassion with the mind's wisdom. If dying people manage their physical pain through medication, caregivers manage their emotional pain through meditation.

Assuming a meditative posture and breathing naturally, we practice letting everything be just the way it is. Experiencing pain in the body, we don't withdraw into thoughts or restless resistance. Instead we remain still and bear witness with the inner eye.

Where is the pain? In the forearm? The hip? What is its quality? Does it feel hot? Is it sharp? Does it pulse or ache or tingle? Under the soft light of our inner gaze the pain that seemed to dominate our body becomes less solid and fixed and we are able to be with it.

We give the same careful attention to any painful thoughts that might arise, observing them and then letting them go. If the thoughts are full of judgments ("I hurt because I am bad" or, perhaps, "I hurt because I am a bad caregiver"), we let these judging thoughts pass. Allowing pain to be pain, we return our attention again and again to the body and the breath.

Over time meditation opens a clear and distinct space between our perception of pain and what our minds say about it. Entering this space we come to know that our pain is not us and that equanimity is. As balance returns, healing takes place.

Home Skill: Doing Comeditation

One of the most effective ways to relieve psychic pain is the simple, calming practice of sharing breaths through comeditation, also known as cross-breathing, or simply "the aahh breath."

The practice was disseminated by Patricia Shelton, founder of the Clear Light Society. It was popularized through the efforts of Richard Boerstler, a psychotherapist based in Massachusetts. The following description is adapted from his explanation.[6]

In comeditation the caregiver becomes more than a helpless observer of a loved one's pain by taking on the active role of guide. The guide sits or stands by the bed and for half an hour vocalizes the soothing sound of "aahh" in synchronization with the person's normal breathing. This clears the mind of troubling thoughts and promotes a restful, meditative state in the patient, and often in the guide as well.

Here's how to do it:

1. The room should be warm and silent and the lights dim. The guide sits or stands near the patient, who is lying faceup in bed with arms and hands at the sides and eyes closed.

2. The guide gives a series of relaxation suggestions, starting with "relax the toes" and moving up the body to the ankles . . . knees . . . hips . . . pelvis . . . stomach . . . chest . . . shoulders . . . neck . . . chin . . . mouth . . . cheeks . . . eyes . . . forehead . . . scalp, and finally the whole body.

3. Addressing the person by name, the guide then introduces what is about to happen with these instructions:

"We are now going to share an ancient method of calming the mind and body. There is nothing to fear. I am going to remain beside you for the entire time. You will not be alone.

"With your eyes closed, pay close attention to the sound of my voice. This is all you have to do, just listen carefully to my voice and follow your own normal breathing. Don't try to breathe in any special way. Let go of everything in the mind and just listen and breathe naturally as we begin together the great sound of 'AAAAAAAAHHHHH-HHH.'"

4. Observing the person's lower chest area, the guide then sounds "aahh" each time the patient breathes out, matching the length of the sound to the length of the exhalation.

5. The person may join in vocalizing "aahh" or simply listen to the guide doing it. Continue for twenty to thirty minutes.

6. If the person's breathing is very rapid, Boerstler suggests that instead of sounding "aahh" the guide count out loud the person's exhalations, going from one to ten and then starting over.

Nine

Taking Care of Feelings

You got to look at things with the eye in your
heart, not with the eye in your head.

—Lame Deer

A s CAREGIVERS we always put the feelings of our patients first—
this is fundamental. But we can't do the work well unless we
acknowledge the raw emotions it stirs in us. Inquiring into our feelings, we learn to live fully.

Feelings are important information about ourselves. They dominate our inner life, yet we're often ignorant of their influence because Western culture teaches us to disregard our feelings and dwell in our thoughts. Rational analysis can't penetrate to the emotional core. The way to understand anger, sadness, and other difficult feelings is to *feel* what we feel.

Working with the dying opens the eyes of the heart. We discover the anger, fear, and sadness we've kept hidden for years. We unlock the parts of ourselves held in bondage, and we set them free with awareness.

A parallel process takes place in our patients. Terminal illness thrusts dying people closer to their emotions. The unique bundle of memories, habits, sensations, moods, experiences, and thoughts we think of as *me* is tied up with strong knots of feeling. Dying unravels this distinct sense of self and lets feelings loose. Medication can accentuate the mood swings. The resulting behavior can seem shockingly out of character. The docile wife and homemaker flies into a rage; the ever-stable father collapses into tears.

Dying people must feel their way to the final surrender. Feelings, not thoughts, are the basic expression of dying. When the pain of dying rubs feelings raw, our acceptance is an effective painkiller. By accepting our patients' emotions, we make them less difficult to bear.

Feelings encourage us to be more intimate in our caregiving. The veteran caregiver Frank Ostaseski tells about a tender moment when he got so caught up in the fear and tension of trying to get a demented friend to the toilet in time that they both ended up on the bathroom floor in laughter, tears, and excrement. "You are trying too hard!" counseled his friend.

Don't try to be anything other than yourself. Dying people expect authenticity. Don't be afraid to express your sadness, fear, or confusion. Relax and let go of any fear of feelings. Meet your fear with mercy. Befriend your feelings by "being their sponsor in an affectionate, nonviolent way," advises the poet-monk Thich Nhat Hanh.[1]

The feelings stirred up by caregiving tell us a lot about ourselves, but that doesn't mean we always act on what we feel. Anger, fear, and sadness shouldn't push us into impulsive words or actions that might do harm to our patients and provoke their distrust. Nor should we harshly confront our feelings with self-critical judgments; this only makes us distrust ourselves.

The best way to work with unwanted emotions is to experience them directly, without saying or doing anything. We contain our reactivity and endure its aches and pains. Slowly, patiently, we let the painful feelings express themselves in our bodies. The noted teacher Charlotte Joko Beck calls this making A Bigger Container.[2] We broaden our relationship to life by expanding the range of what we're willing to live *physically*.

In opening to unpleasant emotional sensations that arise in the course of our caregiving, we create more space in our lives for our patients, and for their feelings. We are able to help them, and to help ourselves.

The method is one of gentling our emotions in the way a wild horse is taught to take commands. We stay in touch—but from a distance. When the bucking bronco starts kicking, we wisely get out of the way. We don't verbalize anything; we don't make any decisions. We just note our mental and physical reactions and step back into a meditative stance. Putting our attention on our breath, we let it rise and fall until the hot moment passes.

Later, in reflecting upon the incident, we strive for clarity by trying to identify what made us so angry, fearful, or sad. What are the hidden issues that need the healing light of awareness? Answering this question we come to know our emotional needs, and we learn how to dance with them. The dance has two steps: we experience, and we observe. We allow ourselves to feel so that we can become conscious of who we are. And we change and grow.

The caregiver's journey goes toward growth. Strong feelings power the transformation. Don't try to resolve the contradictory feelings stirred up by caregiving. Just let the process of your transformation unfold in its own good time.

MEETING EMOTIONAL DEMANDS

Caught in the fiercely personal process of dying, a loved one may vent his feelings often. Unlike a hospital, the home environment presents few social barriers to the expression of feelings. Cognitive impairment can further break down restraint.

Be prepared. As caregiver, you are a convenient target. Try not to take personally any grief, rage, regret, sorrow, or envy your patient directs your way. A loved one's emotional outburst challenges us to understand what's really going on. When we demonstrate in word and deed that her negative feelings are OK, we acknowledge as valid the hurt and frustration that lies underneath.

The primary colors that tint the emotional landscape of the dying are anger, fear, and sadness.

ANGER, A PART OF THE PROCESS

When we work with the dying, anger comes with the territory. The pioneer thanatologist Dr. Elisabeth Kübler-Ross theorized that anger is an essential stage in the dying process. Subsequent research has not substantiated her theory, but dying people do have plenty to get angry about.

✦ The physical and mental pain can be so intense that even good-tempered patients sometimes turn nasty and resistant.

✦ Dying is loss, and loss foments the anger of frustration. The dying person must give up everything: relationships, physical functions, future plans. It seems like nothing can be done about it—except to get angry. (As caregivers we experience this kind of anger when we don't want our patients to die and they do, or we wish they would get it over with and they don't.)

✦ Anger is such an easily accessible emotion that some people use it to blow off feelings of sadness or fear they can't otherwise express.

✦ Freud believed that anger turned inward causes depression. Most dying people must work through depression as a normal part of grieving the loss of life. Mood-lifting, antidepressant drugs impede this process and should be avoided unless depression deepens into a downward spiral. Crying is good, but not if it goes on too long.

Not everything about anger is negative. Anger can be a powerful force for change. Its tremendous energy can concentrate dying people's minds and sharpen their images of what they have to cut through to get to their truth. I've seen people kept alive by their anger. It carried them all the way to the end of their self-investigation and cleared the way for a peaceful dying.

There are so many valid reasons for a dying person to express anger that we should be able to accept it. Nevertheless, sometimes we can't.

Our loved ones' anger can touch us in very tender places. We want only to help, but they fling back violent words or gestures that really hurt, or they express their anger passively by sweetly arousing our guilt about not doing enough for them.

Looking deeply into a patient's anger, we can see the pain and meet it with love, but anger, like fear, is contagious. When someone turns mean-spirited, our own anger may flare up too. Here is a simple meditation-in-action practice that can extinguish the flame of anger.

✦ When you feel a hot flush of anger, note it and softly say, "Anger, anger," to bring the calming power of your attention to bear.

✦ At the same time, relax your lower abdomen by taking a deep breath from the belly. When the belly is soft, anger loses its energy and the dangerous moment that seemed so pressing disappears.

✦ Continue to follow your breath, feeling it rise and fall with your belly. On the inhale, mentally say, "Anger, anger"; on the exhale, say, "Love, love." Within a scant two or three minutes, you'll find some clarity returning.

Sometimes we have to let our anger burn. We simply *must* rail at the injustice of our loved ones' illness and the burden it puts on us, or our unexpressed bitterness will harden our hearts.

When you have to unburden your anger, try very hard not to dump it on your patient. But if you do, don't wallow in regret. Your loved one, and the universe, can absorb an angry outburst. Forgive yourself and move on.

A better way to blow off steam is to share your feelings with old friends who don't mind being yelled at or with your support group. (See the Home Skill section at the end of Chapter 5.) On the other hand, as Thich Nhat Hanh acknowledges, "Pillow-pounding may provide some relief but it is not very long lasting."[3] When we are ready to seek long-term relief from anger, we can channel its energy into tolerance and wisdom by cultivating patience in a systematic way.

ANGER TEACHES PATIENCE

Certain monasteries teach monks that when someone gets mad at them it's simply their turn to receive anger. Imagine what it would mean for the world if this practice were adopted on a global scale. War in its many forms would wither away because the only enemy would be anger and the only way to fight it would be with the weapon of patience. Patience is truly a revolutionary force.

As caregivers we should welcome the anger that erupts in the course of our work because it can teach us patience, and patience can change our lives. Anger moves us to impulsive actions that cause us more suffering, but patience helps us weigh choices carefully and make a wise decision. Anger hotly focuses our minds on only one thing, but patience greatly expands our range of possibilities. Anger strikes out at our lives as they are, but patience finds satisfaction in what we have. Anger undermines our happiness; patience cultivates it. Anger destroys; patience creates. Anger enslaves; patience liberates.

Patience is such a powerful positive force that if no other virtue arose from our caregiving, developing patience would be enough.

Patience has three aspects.

✦ The first is a spirit of forgiveness. Our intention is to completely forgive others, harboring no ill will. When this isn't possible we forgive ourselves and let our forgiveness of others blossom in its own good time. Meanwhile we water the soil with patience, and we wait.

✦ The second aspect of patience is a willingness to remain constant and endure hardship. Patient endurance is not a "stiff upper lip." Rather it is a genuine appreciation of difficulty as an essential part of life. When an ancient master said, "Every day is a good day," he wasn't wearing rosy tinted glasses. He meant that every day is good as it is—a perfect expression of life.

This aspect of patience keeps us present for our loved ones all the way to the end. Expecting nothing, we are patient in the way that simply *is*.

✦ The third aspect of patience is a determination to pursue the truth no matter what. We tend to carry around images of reality that differ from the truth. Rather than see what actually is, we project our own thoughts as the world. We say, for example, that someone "makes" us mad when in fact we are the ones who make up the reasons for our anger.

There is a story about a boatman on a foggy river who gets furious when struck by a passing vessel. Then he discovers that the other boat is empty and there is no one to blame for the accident.

Anger feels solid and dense when it hits us, but soon it passes away, because anger, like everything, is impermanent. At the very moment it surges up, anger begins to recede. If we can patiently wait for the wave to pass, it will rock us only briefly, and we'll be quickly back in balance.

To develop patience, we isolate and study our anger.

First, we step back and give it lots of room. The process is one of opening a mental space large enough to allow anger to dissipate without doing damage. "To give your sheep or cow a large, spacious meadow is the way to control him," says Suzuki-roshi.[4]

Second, we bring our attention to bear, and, in the words of the Buddha, "merely observe." This does not mean detaching. We remain fully engaged with the intense discomfort that anger is causing us. We feel its burning pressure to strike back, but we do nothing. We just watch the soap opera playing in the mind, and we note the unpleasant sensations arising in the body.

As we observe, we identify anger's characteristics. Does the back hurt? Does the forehead pound with pressure? Do the shoulders hunch up?

Studying anger in this way gives us distance from it and diminishes its power. And we make a startling discovery: our anger is not us. Nor is it *our* anger. Anger belongs to no one; anger is just a beach ball that keeps getting bounced around. As we watch it bounce, it disappears. Remaining attentive to our anger, we dispel it. Repeating this practice again and again gives us more tolerance than we ever thought possible.

Receiving anger with patience builds A Bigger Container. We expand the amount of life we're willing to take in without getting upset. But we still have limits. When our cup of anger, fear, or sadness starts to spill over, we need to pour out the troubled contents to a trusted friend.

BEING WITH FEAR

Fear can be an appropriate guide in our lives; it can make us wary when we should be. But no matter how cautious and careful we are, our survival is always at risk because we are destined from birth to die. This terrifying prospect becomes undeniable in terminal illness, and we stiffen against it. We try to block the path to our death with fear.

Although most people die in peace, every dying person I've known has suffered at least a few terrible moments of fear—fear of pain, fear of helplessness, fear of loss. An effective intervention against fear softens this hard wall of resistance. The home care team has many medical and psychosocial tools to help patients let down their fear and relax. The medical staff address physical pain through medication; the social worker pulls together family support; clergy and psychotherapists provide counseling; massage, art, and music therapists do their part; but the caregiver is the expert in the very effective therapy of "being there."

Although there are times when a dying person wants to be alone, no one wants to die feeling isolated and abandoned. Our job as caregivers is to comfort our patients with an abiding sense of accompaniment. No matter how frightening things get, we'll be there.

What being there means is specific to each dying person. Charles, a much-loved patient, was showing signs of paranoia. He was getting weaker and more vulnerable, and he was afraid people wouldn't take care of him as his health deteriorated. Getting to sleep had become difficult for him. His dreams were filled with a terrible longing to escape, and panic attacks were waking him up full of fear. He told volunteers he was desperate to die; he anguished over why it was taking so long. In the midst of all this, a note appeared in the Patient Log.

> Staff suggests that evening shift volunteers should spend some time with [Charles] before he goes to bed. Ask him how his day was, let him ventilate some of his fears and concerns, but don't get him worked up.

This simple suggestion proved to be very effective because it was skillfully crafted just for Charles. As caregivers we continually seek to discover and apply the methods of accompaniment that work best for each particular patient.

Caregivers are not immune to fear. Seeing firsthand the absolute power of death, we may cringe and recoil. This is fear of death. If we care for someone with AIDS we may struggle with fear of contagion. Or we may experience fear of loss and fear of helplessness as we watch a loved one draw away from us.

By practicing lovingkindness we transform our many fears. Lovingkindness is the practice of gently befriending the fear that comes up within us and our patients. This openhearted acceptance is not wimpy or weak. It is strong and unconditional and carries the force of deep friendship. If patience is the way to transform anger, lovingkindness is the way to transform fear.

THE LOVINGKINDNESS MEDITATION

Legend holds that the Buddha devised a special meditation for a group of terrified monks driven out of the forest by fiendish tree spirits. He sent the monks back with phrases of loving forgiveness to recite and practice. In this way they won over the enemy spirits.[5] By reciting these same phrases you can make peace with your own internal demons.

Get in a comfortable position, close your eyes, and let your arms hang heavy and your shoulders droop. Allowing your body to completely relax, let go of your plans and preoccupations and simply follow the rise and fall of your breath. When you feel somewhat quiet inside, allow your attention to drop from the thoughts in your head to your heart, the emotional center. Then repeat over and over to yourself for ten or fifteen minutes these beautiful lines:

> May I be happy.
> May I be peaceful.
> May I have ease of well-being.
> May I be filled with love for the whole world.

The lovingkindness meditation generates a powerful sense of benevolence that touches all those around you. Should you want to include your patient more directly, you can bring his image to mind and then send lovingkindness his way by inwardly saying, "May you be happy," and so forth. You may also wish to do the meditation using additional phrases that carry particular power for you.

It's easy to feel skeptical about such a simple exercise. The entire thrust of our society is toward mentally complex solutions to emotional problems. People seek change through years of talk-centered psychotherapies—how can saying a few childlike phrases make a difference?

The lovingkindness meditation works by stimulating our inherent source of emotional well-being. By repeating the phrases we perform a self-blessing. We gladden the heart and arouse its capacity to soften and neutralize hurtful mental states.

Experience this for yourself by doing the meditation daily for several weeks. You might practice it while you're at the bedside and your patient is resting, or you may prefer to reserve a time when you're completely apart from the pressures of caregiving.

The important thing is to relax. Don't struggle against any feelings that come up; instead let them permeate your body. And if no special feelings arise, just continue doing the meditation. Eventually the armor opens and the heart becomes available to absorb fear and render it harmless. When fear does not intervene, caregiver and patient can heal and grow whole together.

SADNESS AS A SIGN OF GROWTH

In nearing the end of life people often move into greater emotional sensitivity. The fearful mind at last takes refuge in the heart and finds acceptance. People become more open to their own feelings and more receptive to those of others. One of the first fruits of this growth toward tenderness is a willingness to express sadness.

Sadness is a natural part of separating and saying good-bye. Don't be afraid of your loved one's tears. Prolonged depression may require counseling and medication, but in most cases a dying person who is deeply sad wants nothing more than to hold hands quietly or be left in solitude. Blinds and curtains on the windows will allow the patient to vary the light depending on mood.

As caregivers we may expect sadness and grief to take a big toll on us. However, this doesn't usually happen for those who do the work daily and remain busy with the many duties that caregiving imposes. A certain protective denial tends to shield against the full force of difficult feelings.

This helps get the job done, but there is a danger in letting practical tasks dominate the attention. Spiritual development requires a full awareness of feelings. Giving our feelings attention without acting them out is not a comfortable process, but it teaches life-changing lessons.

GROUNDING EMOTIONS THROUGH SENSE SATISFACTION

In dying, the senses fail us one by one. Vision is typically the first to go and hearing the last. Be alert to the state of your patient's senses so you can satisfy them as much as possible. Sense satisfaction can ground dying people in physical reality and draw them away from angry, fearful, and sad mental states. (Conversely, the sensory deficit of stark white hospitals heightens anxiety.)

Touch.

Comfort your loved one with fuzzy blankets; flannel sheets in cold weather; a plastic, rather than a metal, bedpan; sheepskin booties; and, perhaps, the ubiquitous teddy bear. Touch can be a powerful catalyst for releasing emotions: provide gentle massages as described in Chapter 10.

Vision.

Know your patient's color preferences and treat them as seriously as if they were food requests.

Smell.

Flowers, fresh air, and sheets freshened by sunlight are favorites; also try incense, perfume, fragrant lotions, even an electric aroma machine.

Taste.

Give your loved one whatever he craves; dying people don't need diets. This point is further developed in Chapter 7.

Hearing.

Music can be a wonderful medium for evoking emotions and achieving release. The emotional depth and breadth of music create a vast and private space where feelings can safely emerge. And music is an effective therapy for relieving pain, both through distraction and through direct sense satisfaction.

If you have any training in playing a musical instrument, don't be afraid to bring it to your caregiving. Simple tunes played at the bedside will be deeply appreciated. But even if you aren't a musician, low-cost, high-quality sound equipment is now so readily available that music is a therapy accessible to almost everyone.

Keep a wide range of tapes and CDs accessible so your patient can choose the music that fits her mood. Afterward offer to talk with her about what she's feeling.

Most sick people like being read to. Choose books that are also on tape and your loved one can keep on with the book even when you're not around. Wind chimes outside the window can be soothing. And, for your sake, be selective when you choose the bedside bell—that's one sound you'll hear often!

"TAKING AND SENDING"

A powerful meditation practice is becoming popular in America. Caregivers can use it to open their hearts to their patients' strong, destructive feelings. We take in the fear, frustration, pain, rage, guilt, and doubt of another and send back calm, compassionate consciousness.

Here's how to do the visualization practice of taking and sending:

1. Relax and settle into a meditative state. Let your thoughts lose their importance by merging your mind with your breath.

2. Imagine as vividly as possible the face of your dying loved one. See in its features the evidence of loss—the anxiety, the weariness, the painful frustration. Open your heart to your loved one as you watch his suffering rise like hot, grimy smoke.

3. Breathe in this black cloud, letting it enter your nostrils and travel all the way down to your heart. Pause naturally, feel the black cloud dissolve in the purity of your heart, and then, on the outbreath, send back a peaceful white light that fills the dying person with happiness and well-being.

4. See your loved one being changed by this healing and becoming happy and free. Then take in another breath of black cloud. Continue steadily in this way for ten or fifteen minutes.

There is something a little scary about taking and sending. Breathing in black smoke doesn't sound very healthy. But strangely enough those who practice it on a regular basis report that instead of making them sick, taking and sending gives them a wonderful new sense of well-being. By opening their hearts they enlarge their capacity to absorb the direct experience of love. In exchanging the burden of self for the suffering of others, they lighten their lives.

CARING FOR THE CAREGIVER

Because feelings are so strongly personal they compel us to recognize that caregiving is all about relationship. Through empathy we *feel* connected with our patients. We intimately experience the feelings they are having. Our hearts tremble with their joy, and when they hurt, we hurt.

Empathy makes it possible for us to help others, but empathy has its hazards. Accompanying the emotional ups and downs of a dying loved one is an unsettling trip.

Terminal care makes tremendous emotional demands on the caregiver. The body retains the memory of stress long after the mind forgets. Make relaxing physical activity a part of your regular schedule. Do something that feels good and also softens and releases tight muscles. Try swimming, tai chi, yoga, dancing, or long walks in nature. Set up a regular time for a massage or a visit to the chiropractor. Bodywork can do wonders.

If a task or a day or a mood continues to overwhelm, acknowledge it. Try doing something simple for a while. If that doesn't work, stop and write down what you're feeling, or call someone up for a talk, or ask someone to come over and cover for a few hours while you take a break.

Burnout is an issue. Regular time-outs and times off are essential for nurturing the spirit. We need space apart from our work in order to recognize the success we are having, and to be refreshed by it. You are as worthy as your patient. Take care of the caregiver.

As caregivers involved in loved ones' dying and death, we feel a constant tug on our hearts. Sometimes it feels like we have to draw the line. When we're too identified with another person's agony, we can't be of any help. How do we keep our balance and still keep our commitment?

We don't need to retreat from our patients to escape from burnout. As Thich Nhat Hanh says, "Mindfulness is the refuge."[6] In bringing our awareness back to what is right in front of us, we enter an oasis of kindness. By taking a breath *and knowing that we are breathing,* we bathe ourselves with refreshment. Just do one thing. The here and now is empty of stress. Heaven is always at hand. Breathe, breathe, breathe.

One way to relieve feelings is to keep a journal. Try to jot something down every day. A journal is not another caregiving chore but rather your friend of last resort. Don't demand clarity or excellence in expression. Just start by writing, "I feel . . . ," and let the words flow right along with the feelings.

Record stressful events and note your physical and emotional responses. Later you'll find that even a fragmentary record contains important insights you had forgotten or not noticed in the intensity of your caregiving work. Let your journal be a history of your spiritual progress and a guide for later growth through reflection. Use your journal as a record for bringing up personal issues in your support group.

Home Skill: "Deep Roll" Breathing

Walter Truett Anderson describes a simple but powerful technique for evoking and clearing strong emotions through a three-step process of breathing from the diaphragm.[7] This is "deep roll" breathing.

Begin by lying comfortably on your back. Rest one hand lightly on your navel to locate your attention there.

Inhale from the belly.

1. First, raise the belly so that air flows into the lower part of the lungs.

2. Without pausing, let your inhale continue smoothly and allow air to fill the middle of the lung cavity.

3. Finally, bring the breath all the way to the upper part of the lungs and let your shoulders rise naturally.

The exhale is also done in three parts without pausing. Expel the breath slowly and smoothly from first the upper, then the middle, and finally the lower part of the lungs. Your hand will drop when exhalation is complete.

Continue with the deep roll breathing for at least twenty minutes. It can be done slowly to induce relaxation or rapidly, as in Reichian therapy, to release a buildup of tension. As long as the pace is comfortable you won't hyperventilate, Anderson says. "Basically it is a clearing process," he says, "a way of allowing feelings to come up and move out, a release for stored blocks in the nervous system."

Ten

Touch Is the Way to Connect

> There is only one temple in the world, and
> that is the human body.
>
> —Novalis

T HE MIND AND BODY ARE ONE. So many empirical studies have confirmed this truth that mind-body medicine now flourishes as a distinct and successful branch of health care in America. Dozens of therapies enjoining patients to employ their attitudes, thoughts, feelings, and imagination in the healing process have moved into the mainstream. Many others, some quite radical, are poised on the edge of acceptance.

Dr. Larry Dossey, pioneer researcher in the new medicine, believes this represents an important advance over the traditional mechanical model of medicine that arose out of seventeenth-century rationalism. Yet Dossey points out that both mechanical and mind-body medicine restrict therapy to the individual. In his terms, both are *local* in their emphasis.

Dossey identifies a third set of therapies that are *nonlocal*. This "Era III medicine" transcends individual minds and bodies to evoke a larger healing power through prayer, the laying on of hands, or other transpersonal means.[1]

Such practices have been around since antiquity, but that doesn't make them scientific. Still, there is growing evidence that consciousness and matter interact in wondrous, even miraculous ways.

Science, especially particle theory, is exploring previously unthinkable realms. Our bodies may not be finite and bounded after all. Is it too much to suggest that we are one?

All minds become One when we unite with our patients through healing touch. Our hands become the conduit for the universal energy, and the act of getting in touch with it transforms us. Through touch we experience the deeper truth of our intimate connection with everything.

TOUCHING AND BEING TOUCHED

Touch is a basic need. During the traumatic transitions of birth and death we need as much touch as possible. In maternity wards volunteers cuddle premature babies. Caregivers do the same for the dying. Hug, hold, and cuddle your loved one as often as appropriate.

Touch is the essence of caregiving, but there is no single way to do it. Since body and mind cannot be separated, the feeling tone of the touching is as important as where the fingers are placed.

Entrust your mind to Big Mind. Put your faith in your hands and your heart. Let go of any intention to change or fix your patient and simply express support and concern through every finger.

When caring and trust are present, touching encourages healing. Reassuring touch reduces anxiety and fear, lowers the heart and pulse rates, increases relaxation and feelings of well-being, and calms the breath.

Touch is communication; it speaks our acceptance more powerfully than words. Society equates personal worth with a healthy physique; touching lets your loved one know you still care despite his ill health.

The right touch at the right moment acknowledges suffering and reassures patients that they are not alone. Long after your loved one has lost the capacity to engage in verbal exchange, she will understand the love that's expressed with a caring touch and a loving presence.

Being physically in touch with your patient will put you in touch with yourself. It can be a powerful experience to have your hands on your dying loved one's body, especially if it's disfigured by disease. How does this make you feel? Are you fearful? Sad? Loving? Indifferent?

Don't repress your reactions; doing so will only confuse you. Get in touch with your feelings. See them clearly, unclouded by judgment. Then jot down these observations in your journal or discuss them with your support group.

Making the touch connection can sometimes be disconcerting. It still gives me a twinge to recall the first time I put a condom catheter on an incontinent male patient. As its name implies, this type of catheter is simply a condom with a tube at one end that leads to a urine collection bag. An adhesive as sticky as flypaper holds the condom in place. Unfortunately, in my first attempt to roll the condom over my patient's penis I caught the sticky adhesive in his pubic hair. We both winced—a perfect demonstration of compassion, which means "suffering with"!

BRING TOUCH INTO EVERYTHING

Incorporate sensitive touch into all parts of your regular caregiving routine. As you help her make the transfer from wheelchair to bed, or turn her to avoid bedsores, or help her onto the commode, give your loved one a few soothing strokes. Even lightly brushing her hand while changing the sheets or giving a glass of water can send the vital message that she matters.

If disease has made your patient's body unattractive, giving him a bath or a back rub may be better than words for saying that you love him. Doctors and nurses can help make your touch-related treatments better; ask them how to clean a painful sore or remove a bandage in the least painful way.

Although touch is generally helpful, sometimes a little encouragement is in order. Patients initially reluctant to receive back rubs and massages from family members and friends might find it easier to cross this threshold by beginning with a professional masseur.

Massage can relieve pain, reduce the risk of bedsores, increase communication, and enhance the sense of well-being. When giving a massage, begin by asking your loved one where she would like to be touched. Then let your touching evolve naturally. Move slowly and pay attention to what feels comfortable for both of you. Note: Anyone who is having radiation therapy should avoid massage in the treatment area.

Avoid deep massage, which can damage frail skin and bones. Stroke the head, hands, feet, back, or whole body. Use a moisturizing lotion (not an oil or alcohol rub) to soothe skin made dry and itchy by inactivity, drug treatment, or disease. Remember to choose a lotion that has a scent your patient finds acceptable. Put the lotion on your hands first to warm it and prevent friction. A hospital bed you can raise and lower electronically offers easier access.

Have the person relax by gazing at a comforting object or by closing her eyes and following her breathing or by imagining a peaceful scene. As you stroke her, be sensitive to the feel of the skin and the way she reacts to your hands. Use this opportunity to learn more about your patient so you can help her. "Read" any changes in her physical condition. Note fluctuations in breathing, changes in temperature, or a rise or fall in pulse rate.

Touch can release powerful emotions embedded in the body. Your hands may prompt a gusher of tears and memories, and your loved one may want to talk about deeply personal things. (Lying with the face turned away during massage seems to make it easier for some people to talk intimately because there is no eye contact.)

Be ready to encourage your patient to use these moments to make peace with his life. Keep a tape recorder handy to support him in his storytelling if this is something he wants. Of course you should always ask permission before turning on the recorder, or doing any other procedure. Respect invites openness and trust. The act of asking makes you more mindful and increases your enjoyment of the moment.

RANGE-OF-MOTION EXERCISES

People lying in bed for long periods of time tend to stiffen into fixed postures. Range-of-motion exercises promote flexibility and provide a pleasant way for patient and caregiver to share a hands-on experience. The patient relaxes, and the caregiver gently lifts and slowly moves each body part in all possible directions around the joint.

These exercises were developed for those who could no longer move their own limbs. I've found that patients at all levels of function derive a warm sense of well-being from entrusting their bodies to someone else for a while. Try it with a friend and you'll see.

A good time to do range-of-motion exercises is following a bed bath. Afterward patients often relax into sleep. Here is how to progressively relax body parts.

✦ Begin, as always, by describing the procedure you are about to do. Explain that you will support the full weight of each body part and that all your loved one has to do is relax. If she seems to need to talk, encourage her to silently count her breaths from one to ten, beginning again for as long as the session lasts. Of course the patient should always tell you right away if any movement brings pain. Then move around behind her and assume a comfortable stance that doesn't strain your shoulders or lower back.

✦ Warm your hands, slide a pillow under your loved one's upper back to give support, and start doing the exercises. Begin with the head. Hold it gently in your two hands and lift and move it very slowly from side to side and forward and back, then rotate it from left to right. Tell the person to imagine that the tension is draining away from the head and shoulders. Ask her to feel the head and shoulders relaxing.

Repeat these head movements several times, making sure to provide the head with a full support that gives a sense of safety and trust.

✦ After you work with the head, apply the same technique to the arms, moving them through the range of what the shoulders and elbows will allow. Then do the wrists, fingers, and thumbs. Next do the legs, rotating them around the hips and knees, and conclude with the ankles and toes.

SKILLED TOUCH

The most important quality we bring to our touch is a willingness to concentrate and be fully present. Skilled touch is not a technique; it is paying attention and doing what comes naturally when we are deeply attuned to our patients. When you "listen" to a person's body with a focused mind, your hands know what to do.

The skin is a borderland. As a sensory organ it opens us to the outside, but as a protective membrane it guards our interior against invasion. In approaching patients, we should enter this transitional zone with great care.

The pioneer massage practitioner Irene Smith advises beginning by moving slowly. Give the other person's skin time to sense the approaching hand and register its intention to touch. Even after contact is made, the pace of the massage should be slow and careful. In giving skilled touch we seek to calm and reassure rather than stimulate.

The following are guidelines for giving skilled touch to the dying:

✦ Begin by washing your hands. When doing bodywork on someone with AIDS, be especially careful to wash your hands and fingers thoroughly by scrubbing vigorously with soap. Gentle friction is part of the microbiocidal action.

✦ Make sure the room is warm and draft-free. Place the person on his stomach or side, facing away from you, and uncover only that portion of the body that you intend to massage.

✦ Focus your thoughts on the love that you feel for the person. Do a minute or two of the lovingkindness meditation in Chapter 9. Relax and open your mind to Big Mind. As you meditate, watch the rise and fall of your loved one's breath and synchronize your breath with his.

✦ Warm your hands by rubbing them together. Then: (1) gently lay all five fingertips on the skin, letting the fingertips rest there for a moment without pressure or movement; (2) lower the palm of your hand and let the whole hand rest; and (3) begin lightly stroking or doing other hand movements.

✦ Use long, sweeping strokes to soothe and relax. Avoid areas of broken skin or acute inflammation and varicose veins. Be careful to rub around, rather than on, bony prominences. Give special attention to reddened areas where circulation has been impaired by pressure and bedsores are possible. Gently knead the skin surrounding these areas.

✦ You may gently apply more pressure, particularly on the upward strokes, if this helps relax the muscles, but the general rule in working with the dying is the less the better. Painful areas can be acknowledged by simply laying on your hand without pressure or movement.

✦ Adjust the length of the session to the patient's state of health. For those in the later stages of illness, any more than fifteen minutes of massage may deplete their energy.

✦ In ending the session, depart from the skin in the same mindful way that you approached: rest the hands quietly, lift them gently, and then leave the energy field smoothly. Irene Smith notes, "Every cell in the human body has consciousness and, therefore, deserves to be treated with the utmost dignity and respect."[2]

✦ Afterward wash your hands again thoroughly. This will clear any energy buildup you may have accumulated and guard against transmission of germs.

Don't be overly concerned about giving skilled touch to someone infected with HIV. The virus is fragile and not easily transmitted, but it is essential to wash your hands thoroughly both before and after.

INTIMATE TOUCH

For dying people in a relationship, intimate touch can enrich the quality of life. Many couples have sex together until only a few weeks before one of them dies. Making it possible for couples to share quiet, uninterrupted time may require some planning and co-ordination by the caregiving team.

When the couple is of the same sex, there may be objections from family members. It can be helpful to focus discussion on the dying person's right to autonomy. If there is conflict, talk it over with your support group or seek mediation by counselors. The effort is worth it. Getting through this difficult passage may lead to a larger reconciliation that deepens everyone's understanding.

The stress and pain of terminal illness tend to dampen a person's interest in having sexual relations, but that doesn't mean sexuality ceases. Patients can still be touched in ways that show they are loved and desired. Holding, stroking, caressing, and quiet talking are effective means for expressing and sharing intimate touch.

Home Skill: Caring for the Feet

The feet are a good place to begin developing a regular practice of massage. Most people are not threatened by having their feet touched, and this is a quick way for a rushed caregiver to make physical contact.

 • Massage relieves feet made cold, numb, or swollen from lying prone for long periods. (The feet depend on activity for proper circulation.) To stimulate the blood flow through the feet, also massage the calf and thigh and do range-of-motion exercises by flexing, extending, and gently twisting the knees, ankles, and toes. Afterward put on booties or warm socks without elastic tops that can block the circulation.

• The feet are great fun to pamper. Wash the person's feet with warm (not hot) water. Use a soft sponge or washcloth and pretend you're bathing a baby. The feet can then be rubbed vigorously with a dry towel. After the feet are dry, apply a lanolin lotion to keep them soft.

• Keep the toenails trimmed. Long toenails and calluses cause discomfort and can make walking difficult. Clip the toenails straight across, but never cut corns or calluses. Before attempting to remove calluses, soften them by wrapping the feet in warm, wet towels. The dead skin will then come off more easily. Use a pumice stone to remove whatever remains.

The feet have nerve endings from the whole body. Reflexology is based on a belief that all glands and organs of the body are represented by points in the feet and hands. This is explained in foot charts that can be incorporated into massage.

Eleven

A Death in the Family

We need, in love, to practice only this:
letting each other go.
—Rainer Maria Rilke

W HEN SOMEONE DIES BEFORE HIS TIME, we tend to call it a
tragedy. Yet I can't regard Brian Toole's premature passing as
anything other than perfect because it was so completely shared by
his many friends and family members. Throughout Brian's tortuous
struggle to stay alive, they stayed with him. Among his last moments, I was present for this one, which I recorded in my journal.

He sits upright in bed, comatose, surrounded by those who
love him. Warmhearted Melissa, caregiver and confidante,
strokes his hand. Opposite proudly sits his brother Joe, here
from Massachusetts. When I introduce myself, Joe smiles and
shows what family means to him by pulling out a picture of
his four kids.

Sister Rosemary, who has talked with Brian every single day
of these last difficult years, rests in a hotel nearby, using the
room of their mother, Marie, who just flew in from Florida.
Other siblings are in touch and on the way here from everywhere.

We camp around Brian's frail presence, warmed by him and
by each other. After a while Melissa, radiant, gets up and
streams out, promising a soon return. Almost immediately
Dean, who has driven his bike down from Sacramento,

clumps in wearing boots, gives Brian a kiss, sits down, starts stroking the very same hand Melissa had held.

Then mother Marie enters, and Joe cedes to her the privileged chair by the bed. She is composed, relaxed, pleasant. When she tells me she's pleased to meet me, I really believe it. This is a very special occasion. Brian has made it happen; his dying has let us see in each other the very thing that is most important to us all. Hearts tender and open, we know that bliss is real. So real, and yet so rare. So rare.

This chapter is about family—the families we're born into, the families we create for ourselves through love and friendship, and the families that come together at the bedside of a dying person.

Not everyone has the good fortune to be born into a family as loving and supportive as Brian Toole's. Many people must enter the world through families full of problems. Others have no family at all. But there is one big family we all belong to—the great body of beings who come into, and pass out of, existence.

Death identifies us with every person and every thing. Because everything changes, we are one with everything. It's a world full of relatives, but only rarely do we feel our universal kinship.

Caregiving connects us with the family of birth and death. We find our place in the order of things by caring for loved ones and then letting them go. Through it all we unburden our hearts to those close to us. Family comes together as a family member moves away. Letting go brings a sense of belonging.

ALL FORMS OF FAMILY

Today family can be almost any combination of people. It may be based on ties of blood and marriage, or it may be more a matter of choice, as in strong networks of friends or intentional communities.

Sometimes illness builds family-style friendships. The dying person may become very close to a fellow member of a cancer patient support group or to a volunteer. These are profound relationships which birth families should honor.

The only essential ingredients for family are an enduring commitment and a sense of mutual obligation. Family does not disown family.

Typically, home care has been the work of one or two family members who lived with, and were related to, the dying person. A couple would bring into their home an ailing parent, for example, or one spouse would care for the other. Neighbors and relatives helped out. Medical support and clergy were called in as needed.

This model still prevails, but there are also new options. The many forms of family have broadened the pool of potential caregivers. At the same time, home care services have become more widespread and specialized.

As a result, these days a sister might care for a dying brother in his home while living with her husband and their family elsewhere. When she can't be with her brother, his close friends ("family") assist. A nurse checks in on a regular basis.

In the best situations, the dying person's many family members come together in a seamless circle of care, as happened for Brian Toole. A good family or support group process at death can leave all involved feeling good about themselves, each other, and the person who died. Most people in families and friendship networks are very glad they cared for their dying loved ones instead of letting them die in a hospital. There is less to grieve when we know we did all we could.

THE UNIT OF CARE

Like birth, death occurs in relationship with those around us. Dying people need to share their pain and suffering because sharing gives meaning to the experience. We find meaning in meaning something to someone else.

Most cultures honor this truth by making death a normal part of community life. In America death is more hidden, and its sharing usually takes place within the dying person's inner circle. That's why we define the unit of care as the patient plus her or his family or strong network of colleagues, neighbors, and friends.

The family also needs care. The stress of a death is often greater on the family than on the dying person. The pressure of caregiving comes on top of the hectic demands of daily life. Although everyone pitches in and helps, the loved one continues to decline. Doubt grows. Can the family survive this death? To ease their fear and grief, family members need to talk, talk, talk. And they need to be heard without judgment.

Families receive care from several sources.

✦ Home care professionals and trained volunteers help family members cope with the many practical and emotional tasks thrust upon them.

✦ Family members help each other. The family with good communication knows how to apply around the kitchen table the listening skills developed at the bedside. The hurt and helplessness of the death need to be shared by everyone.

✦ The patient can be a source of comfort and enlightening information. Many dying people consciously want to help those around them. Others help simply by sharing the experience of death. The patient is an integral part of the caregiving team.

SUPPORT THE PRIMARY CAREGIVER

Within the caregiving circle, the primary caregiver is at the center. The primary caregiver is usually the spouse, partner, child, or sibling who takes charge of ensuring that the day-to-day caregiving gets done.

This is a deeply challenging duty. Not only do primary caregivers face losing someone they love—or toward whom they may have deeply conflicted feelings—but they may get little credit from relatives and friends less intimately involved.

Those in the wider caregiving circle should do all they can to support the primary caregiver in practical ways. They can shop for food, cook meals, provide transportation, pick up prescriptions, return phone calls from those who want to know how the patient is ("did he die yet?"), offer child care, and on and on.

It's vitally important to schedule regular times when alternate caregivers step in and give the primary caregiver time-outs and times off. These may be anything from going to the movies or taking a hike to attending worship services or seeing a grief counselor. Periodic respite is more than a way to relieve stress; it's a spiritual necessity. The heavy physical and emotional demands of caring for a dying person can exhaust awareness.

Primary caregivers may have to be pushed to take a break. Their work is so compelling they may not want to stop, even briefly. What if she needs me? a silent voice keeps asking. What if he dies? Sometimes the voice isn't so silent. A dying person can get very needy and may complain loudly when the primary caregiver tries to leave the house.

The pressure can get a little crazy-making. The best way to vent explosive feelings of anger and resentment is by talking them over with others. Friends and loved ones can be sympathetic listeners, but primary caregivers face special problems. The best listening ears belong to those sharing the same difficult experience.

Primary caregivers need to talk with primary caregivers. Many national organizations for specific diseases, county and municipal government social service agencies, and local health-related nonprofit organizations maintain support groups for primary caregivers.

DON'T WITHHOLD THE TRUTH

Our deepest relationships intertwine with our deepest sense of meaning. That's why family and close friends have a vital role to play in confirming to the patient that death is imminent. The social acknowledgment of death reduces its isolating impact, helps patients abandon the false hope of healing through physical recovery, and facilitates their internal work of accepting death and enjoying their last days to the fullest.

If dying loved ones have been involved in a long fight for life against illness, it may be difficult for family members to shift over to helping them die. But it is important to do this out of love. When we truly love people, we don't deny them the truth.

Sometimes family members withhold the bad news because they are afraid their loved ones will lose hope and die sooner. But this isn't how it works. Ask anyone with experience, and you'll be told that when people are dying, they usually know it. If they don't say anything, it's probably because they sense that others can't handle it. The result is a shadow play, with each side presenting a falsely optimistic face.

This can put a terrible strain on a dying person. At death we long for authentic communication. There is no time to waste on pretense. When a loved one is dying, we should gently confirm that we know. And we should do it in a way that doesn't rob the dying person of hope. The hope caregivers can offer is the firm commitment to stay with our loved ones to the end.

HEALING THE FAMILY

Death is a time of great potential for family renewal. Dying isn't grounded in the expectations and histories of existing relationships. The powerful immediacy of the experience can break the chains of conditioned response and let loose new freedom between family members. Words are suddenly found for things long left unsaid. Families come together.

I've seen people who wouldn't talk to each other for years holding hands at the bedside. In one remarkable case family members achieved reconciliation on a long-distance call while the telephone was being passed back and forth over the dying person in bed.

Dying opens the heart and makes us sensitive to the ways we have hurt others. Righting these painful wrongs can be an important task of the dying. As caregivers we should always be on the lookout for evidence that our patients ones need to reconcile past hurts and complete unfinished business.

If the person feels she has aggrieved someone in the family, we can offer to set up a meeting or phone call. When the person is too timid or weak to undertake this challenge, we can write down what he wants to say. Then we can read it over the phone to the aggrieved person and report back the response.

Sometimes the dying person feels blocked in her relationship with someone who is absent or deceased. Try having her visualize that person and then have a reconciliation conversation with him. Or have her write the person a letter which is then burned in a ceremony. A therapist will have other suggestions; ask your hospice for a referral.

When dying people achieve resolution, the shift is apparent to anyone who works mindfully with them. It can appear as a tenderness in their tone or a new kindness in the way they treat everyone around them. Or it may be a brilliance that shines in the eyes, as if they see through their illness to a peace that is beyond pain and death.

As caregivers many of us feel that our biological families have failed us. We may see family as more of a hindrance than a help. We may want to avoid destructive patterns developed over years of miscommunication. Divorce and remarriage may have added extra confusion to long-standing conflicts. There may be many regrets about the way things were done in the past. There may be many fears about how the impending death will affect the family's future. The whole thing might feel so painful that we are tempted to forsake family entirely.

When we have the courage to face the family issues that dying raises, we make transformation possible. It takes courage to commit to caring for dying family members from whom we've been estranged. It takes courage to include in the caregiving circle family members who have been sources of pain for us or our dying loved ones. It takes courage, and it takes heart.

A loved one's dying can open the hearts of family members grown cold over the years. The pain and suffering of the dying person can raise the tender hope of having a strong, loving family. Like sitting around a fire as it fades into coals, caring for a dying family member draws people together.

If the family remains locked in misunderstandings, ask the hospice social worker to help. A good facilitator can help clear out the aversion, fear, sense of inadequacy, and outright denial that block patient, friends, and family members from moving toward resolution.

AIDS AND THE FAMILY

It's wonderful when everyone joins hands in a healing circle. Unfortunately, the news that someone in the family is dying of AIDS sometimes triggers a hurtful response. HIV infection is a social as well as a medical issue. The fear and shame society attaches to the disease because of its association with homosexuality and drug use can have a profound emotional impact on the family.

If the family pulls away, the dying person suffers an enormous sense of loss. Acceptance by one's family has unique importance. Anything we can do to unite biological families divided by the issue of AIDS affirms this great healing hope: "May all beings be happy; may they be joyous and live in safety."

THE CAREGIVER AS HOST

Most dying people want and need visitors. Dying is a social event, and caregivers are the social secretaries. It's not easy work.

Locating scattered relatives and friends can take time. Tenderly conveying the news may be even more difficult. (If there are many people to contact, get others to help.) Describe the person's condition, answer any questions, and explain why a visit is important. Be prepared for people to arrive just when you're too tired to deal with them.

The caregiver plays host to visitors in different stages of accepting the situation. Some are genuinely helpful, and some are not. Our society doesn't prepare people for death. Seeing it close up can spark a variety of inappropriate responses.

Friends and family may show up determined to wear a happy face. This becomes a draining experience for a dying person if, for example, the visitors put on happy music and the patient is in a plaintive mood. It can work the other way, too. Sometimes the patient wants to have a good time but the visitors arrive seeking emotional catharsis and push sadness in a way that makes the dying person feel alienated and alone.

Behind these obvious behaviors are complex psychologies. Fearful visitors may blame the dying person for his fatal illness to distance themselves from it. The adult children of dying parents may respond out of guilt, blaming themselves for the demise of Mom or Dad. Sometimes a parent is overly protective of a dying child; sometimes an in-law or close friend feels shut out of the inner circle.

And so it goes. The teeter-totter of conflicting emotional needs can exhaust the conscientious caregiver. Home care staff can help, but ultimately we have to find our own balance.

At the very moment you feel pressure building, drop your attention to your breath as it rises and falls in the belly. "Seen" from the center of the body, everything comes into perspective. The heavy expectations of visitors fall away, and you are able to refocus on your patient. Firmly based in your breath, you convey a reassuring confidence. Your calm presence tells visiting family members and friends just what caregiving is all about. You show by example how they can help.

TIPS FOR VISITORS

Encourage visitors, but plan to fit them into the patient's regular rhythm of eating, cleaning, and sleeping. (Don't forget to keep the patient clean and the room aired out; odors are isolating.) Suggest that regular but short visits are better than infrequent, long, soul-searching sessions.

✦ If the dying person has little energy and can see only close relatives and friends, you will need to discourage others from visiting without hurting their feelings. Have the dying person send cards to those not in the inner circle so they feel remembered and can achieve closure.

✦ For local visitors, try setting regular times for serving tea or juice at the bedside so they can drop in proceeded by nothing more than a phone call. This can evolve into a sustaining ritual, with the person bathing and getting dressed up for the occasion. Or it may become burdensome and have to be abandoned. Ask everyone to stay flexible.

✦ Occasional visitors need to be briefed about the person's condition. Give them an introduction to the landscape of dying. The familiar conditions of home tend to conceal the seriousness of a fatal illness. Make it clear that the person *is* dying.

✦ Reassure those who haven't been around the dying that it's normal to have fears about death. At the same time, warn them not to assume that the dying person shares their fears.

✦ Advise visitors that dying people want to live as much as they can. (They aren't dead yet!) Organize ways visitors can celebrate life with the patient. Bedside parties are great; bring out favorite foods, balloons, songs, and cameras. But be careful about pushing too much good cheer if the person's mood is different. Go with the flow.

✦ It helps to have a list of practical tasks for visitors who simply can't sit still, but try not to overorganize. Leave space for the spontaneity that lets friends and loved ones contribute their creative energy to the caregiving effort.

✦ You might suggest that first-time visitors bring a gift; this will give them something to focus on while they adjust to the patient's changed situation. Flowers are always appropriate. (Plants are not, because they require care.) Other possibilities are pretty notions, such a colorful hair ribbon (unless the person has lost a lot of hair), nail polish, warm socks; a fancy nightgown or funny pajamas, a lap robe for sitting up, a bed jacket, a small, framed reproduction of a restful photograph or painting (the impressionists are popular).

Here are some do's and don'ts for visitors:

Do reflect on that fact that dying is everyone's destiny; **don't** feel sorry for the dying person.

Do try to make the person more comfortable; **don't** try to cure her.

Do keep the conversation located in the here and now; **don't** initiate talk about the future.

Do be as honest as possible without being blunt; **don't** offer false hope.

The most vital skills are learning to relax and listen. Encourage visitors to let the patient control the conversation while they do nothing other than settle in at the bedside and accept whatever comes up.

SIGNS OF APPROACHING DEATH

If the illness has been prolonged, distant visitors may have come and gone. The caregiver may be unsure about when to call them back for the final days. Ask the hospice nurse for an assessment.

Although people do not die in predictable ways, there are clear signs of approaching death.

✦ Interest in conversation declines, and pulse is sluggish. The person wants only to be lightly touched or left alone to reflect or sleep.

✦ Appetite ebbs away. Everything is refused except a little soft food and occasional sips of liquids.

✦ The pain that required medication becomes less pressing.

✦ Control over bladder and bowels is lost.

✦ The person is so weak he may not be able to roll over in bed or lift his head.

SHARING THE LAST DAYS

By now the word is out that death is imminent. Each family member or friend will have to decide whether or not to be present when it happens. Those who decide not to come shouldn't be regarded harshly by those who do. Our hurried, complex lives leave little time for grief. In any case, grieving is an intensely personal experience and can't be judged from the outside. It doesn't help the dying person to have someone present who would rather be elsewhere.

Visitors who weren't present over the course of the person's gradual physical deterioration may be shocked to find her in a weak and wasted state. Even regular caregivers may be frightened if the patient falls into a coma, experiences muscle jerking, or lies with open eyes fixed in a vacant stare.

Watching the final stages of a loved one's death can be agonizing for those unprepared to witness a radical change. Nameless fears may challenge confidence built up over weeks or months of caregiving. You may have thoughts of transferring your patient to a hospital for the actual death.

Fear not. Take a breath and trust yourself. Love and intuition got you this far; they will carry you through to the end. As friends and relatives gather, let the compassion you've cultivated with your patient extend to all those now present.

When anxiety builds as death draws near, try to remember that what we see is not all there is. Form is not the same as content.

Watching a loved one actively die, we should look beyond the body to the internal changes.

We in the West are only in the primitive stages of investigating the unseen. The documentation of thousands of near-death experiences suggests there is much to explore. Many religious traditions believe that some form of consciousness lingers after death. At the very least we should be willing to acknowledge that although death appears absolute, life does not dissipate instantly. If a photograph of an empty parking lot can show the energy forms of cars once parked there, it seems improbable that human beings flick off like light switches. Hair and fingernails continue to grow after death—what other growth processes go on?

Even without a flash of blue light or a flutter of angel wings, the mystery is present and can be felt with an open heart.

PATIENT CARE IN THE FINAL HOURS

As death draws near, the urge to "do something" may grow very strong. Helping a loved one at death is not a matter of what we do but how we are. Being there completely with a calm, loving presence is enough. We know from near-death experiences that even if a person is in a coma the loving presence of others is strongly felt.

Since hearing is one of the last senses to go, *carry on all conversations as if your loved one can hear.* Talk calmly and with assurance; the sound of the voice can give great comfort. Say who is present. Share news about the day. Sometimes energy resurges and the dying person suddenly wants to socialize. Many people say a few words right up to the last moment. Create a reassuring atmosphere by reading a sacred text aloud as a group or playing soft music.

As always, *silent touch is the best way to connect.* Keep it simple. Hold the person's hand or lightly stroke the arm or head. If decreased oxygen to the brain is causing restlessness, a back rub may help quiet your loved one down.

If she is very agitated and insists on getting up even though she is too weak to stand, restrain her in bed to prevent falls. A nurse can explain how to make a restraint system out of folded sheets or strips of gauze bandage.

If the person feels hot, cool washcloths can be applied to the forehead, face, and body. Perspiration-soaked bedclothes can be changed if the person is uncomfortable, but it's best to *disturb as little as possible*. Turning to prevent bedsores is no longer necessary.

The patient's skin may feel cool as blood circulation begins to center on the last vital functions of the heart and lungs. The change in circulation can darken the skin or give rise to purplish blotches on the legs or arms. Put on plenty of warm blankets. Some sources advise against using an electric blanket because of the danger of skin burns.

The need for food and liquid will have greatly diminished or disappeared altogether. *Don't force the dying person to eat or drink.* This is very important. Be alert to any difficulty in swallowing; at this time there is a high risk of choking or getting food into the lungs. When using a syringe to supply water, be careful to inject only a few drops at a time. If the person can suck, ice chips are a pleasant way to relieve dehydration.

Breathing may be irregular and require a lot of effort. Sometimes breathing is accompanied by a moaning sound. This is probably caused by air passing over very relaxed vocal cords and does not indicate pain. *If breathing is difficult, elevate the head of the bed and prop up the person with pillows.* Relieve the dryness caused by mouth breathing with swabs moistened in mineral oil or water.

When breathing is accompanied by a rattle or gurgle, the person is having trouble clearing saliva and secretions that are collecting in the back of the throat. Humidifying the air with a cool mist vaporizer may help loosen dry and encrusted secretions. Offer water in small amounts to keep the mouth and throat moist. Placing the patient on her side while supported by pillows encourages drainage. The hospice nurse may have other suggestions.

PERMISSION TO DIE

It's said that "death is certain, but the hour is uncertain." This may be generally true, but even in the midst of uncertainty many people seem to have some degree of control over the exact moment of death.

Several people I've known hovered on the edge of dying until a loved one could arrive from somewhere far away. Others, it seems, have waited to die until they were left alone. For this reason Dale Borglum of the Living/Dying Project sometimes tells people, "I'm going for a break now. I'll be away for fifteen minutes, just in case you want to die."

We need to give our loved ones permission to die. Throughout most of the dying process, they may find it hard to accept that we will go on living without them. Then, as active dying intensifies, there may come a time when they are ready to get on with it but we won't let them go.

Watching people go through the final moments of dying can be terrifying if we aren't prepared to witness a radical change. As they drift in and out of consciousness, the sight of their inert bodies may cause us to weep.

Dying people sense the agony of friends and family. It pains them to think their deaths are causing hardship for others. Desperate emotions expressed at the deathbed can make departure more difficult.

We ease our loved ones' way by relinquishing our emotional hold on them. Because we don't want our loved ones to suffer, we assure them that we can carry on. We tell them that nothing remains unfinished; we lovingly say good-bye. And we sincerely let them go.

This should be done in a very clear and direct way. Sit down by the bed, bring your mind to the breath to restore a sense of peace, and put your face very close to your loved one's. Then, in heartfelt words full of love, tell him he is dying and the time has come to separate.

Death is a noble moment. We honor our loved one's lives by giving them a loving and dignified departure. This is our great and final gift.

THE MOMENT OF DEATH

At death the mouth may fall open and the eyes may be in a fixed stare with the pupils dilated. When death is suspected, a feeling of panic may arise. Resist any impulse to call emergency services. If you need to talk to someone, call the nurse. Many states do not require notification of police in case of death; all that's needed is a physician's signature. Often it's not even necessary to have the patient officially pronounced dead.

Death has occurred when

✦ There is no breath.

✦ There is no heartbeat.

✦ The person can't be aroused by shaking.

✦ Any waste matter in the bladder or rectum is released.

A POEM

Brian Toole died in Maitri Hospice just before dawn. Afterward Melissa Kay wrote this poem.

To Brian, In the Garden

As the pale morning star surrenders her light
into the radiance of the rising sun,
so have you vanished from our outer sight
into the source—the source of all light:

into the source you so faithfully sought
through sickness, through pain,
through loneliness, through death;

into the warmth of the world's deep heart—
love of all love,
life of all life,
light of all light.

You who have penetrated, lift us now,
that we, too, may enter into the light.
There may the love that we found in life live—
now and now and now and now

Home Skill: Bathing the Body

Keeping the body at home after death will help make the loss real. The period of time is up to you, but three days is common practice. Check on your state law well in advance. In most cases medical or civil authorities don't need to be notified until you're ready for the body to be removed. If your loved one has died in a hospital, it should be possible to get the body home; your hospice program ought to be able to help.

When the body is kept at home, it can become the center of a ceremonial parting that includes periods of meditation, prayer, readings, and music. Ceremonies help us express our loss in a way that goes beyond words. "We seem to be able to access a deeper part of ourselves through ritual than by ordinary discourse," says Charles Garfield.[1]

Washing the body can be a beautiful ritual involving all close friends and family members. Activate your phone tree to get people assembled.

Here are some guidelines for bathing the body.

1. Set up a table in the bedroom to serve as a temporary altar. Drape the table with a dark cloth and place on it a candle, a sacred image, and a stick of burning incense. You may also want soft music.

2. Prepare a bathing solution of warm water and sweetly scented herbs. You might want to try yerba santa, which has a musky, heavy scent. (Have the herbs, candles, incense, and other items for the bathing ritual previously assembled and stored with the last set of clothes, which the loved one may wish to choose.)

3. Using washcloths dipped in the herb water, clean the body head to toe. If the herbs are packaged in cheesecloth packets, you can also use these to lightly rub and scent the body.

4. Change the sheets and linens.

5. Dress the body in something the patient liked, cover it from the waist down, and fold the hands across the chest.

6. Put flowers or a cherished object under the folded hands.

7. Bring everyone together around the body, and form a circle by holding hands.

8. Have someone say a few words or repeat together a chant or prayer which several people know. Unless the person wanted something special done, such as saying the rosary, let spontaneity prevail at this poignant moment. There will be adequate opportunity in the memorial service for prepared readings and statements.

Twelve

Passing through the Gateway of Grief

> Beyond a certain point there is no return.
> This point has to be reached.
>
> —Franz Kafka

CAREGIVERS' WORK doesn't end when our loved ones die. Having faithfully borne witness to the death, it now becomes our task to remain open to our grief. This can be a terrible moment. No matter how slowly the process of dying unfolds, the fact of death always seems to come frighteningly fast. When we feel deeply about someone, the hurt of his loss is always more than we can anticipate. I learned that when Lawrence died. The following is taken from my journal.

Lawrence was a very private and dignified man whose tragic life touched everyone in the hospice. When he died abruptly, we were stunned. People were on the phone immediately, passing the word, passing the word.

My call came during dinner, and I went right away. Two other volunteers were there with Lawrence. Together we sat in the twilight, his small body floating in the bed's vast space. Then more people arrived. A young woman, a new volunteer, came in crying and desperately threw herself down on his bed. As the room began to fill, I went to the kitchen to help prepare meals for patients.

My kitchen chores done, I lit some candles and went back to spend time with Lawrence. Although he had been dead for only two hours, his skin was already cold. When I placed a kiss on his forehead, my lips made a smacking sound in the stillness.

Returning to the Center I sat in the dark courtyard wanting to cry—or something. Finally I went over and hugged a rock bench as if it were Lawrence, or the earth, or myself. As I let go, I felt myself falling to rest.

In learning to take care of the dying, I learn to take care of myself. It hurts to let go, but it hurts more to hold on.

Caregiving is good preventive medicine. Our intimate involvement with dying makes death less of a shock. But that doesn't mean there is no pain. Like all other survivors of loss, caregivers have grief work to do.

In a sense, caregiving makes the grief worse. By taking care of people we deepen our involvement with them. While we're doing it, the work inspires us, but when they're gone and all the bedside duties are done, nothing distracts us from the pain of the loss.

The pain can be brutal, even lethal. Grief is a survival issue. People do indeed die from broken hearts. Surviving spouses run a high risk of not making it through the first year of bereavement, and unresolved grief can set the stage for serious illness later on.[1] It hurts to let go, but it hurts more to hold on.

We want our hurt to come and go as quickly as a thunderstorm, but what we want is often not what we get. It may seem unfair, but grieving, like dying, takes as long as it takes, and the work can be laborious and lengthy.

The work of grief is remaining open to the pain so the wound can heal. There are ways to promote healing, but ultimately it's a matter of letting go and letting it flow. Grief rages through our lives until at last the roaring river exhausts itself in our acceptance. Thus, at the end of our caregiving, as at the beginning, acceptance is everything.

A SPIRITUAL OPENING

Grief's deepest, wildest pain flows from the fear that when a loved one dies, love itself dies. This profound misperception is rooted in the way the human brain works.

The brain reports a purely material world. Sampling the world through the senses, the brain tells us that what we see, smell, taste, touch, and hear is all there is. Other people seem to exist apart from us as separate objects. Love seems to come from outside ourselves, so when we lose a loved one we think we have lost love itself.

Intuition, however, suggests another story. Over the millennia, a persistent inner voice has whispered to humanity that our apparent separation is not real because minds are connected in one. This one Mind is perceived not through the senses but through meditation, prayer, and various mindfulness practices. "The essence of all spiritual practice," writes the English monk Ajahn Amaro, "is to look beyond the sensory world."[2]

Beyond the dominion of the sensory world lies a vast inner realm, and grieving is a gateway to it. By staying with the pain of grief, we cut through our apparent separation from others and open a sixth sense that connects inner and outer.

Science, through quantum physics and the theory of evolution, asserts the unity and interconnection of all things. Caregivers experience this truth in palpable ways. At the deathbed the boundaries of the self get porous, and love moves freely in all directions. We feel the presence of a shared true nature. This comforts us when the loved one is gone because we find that death has brought us closer to others.

Having lost a loved one, we come to value that which is never lost—our integration with everything and everyone. Tolerating grief's intensity leads to a larger, more loving life. "When you touch your pain," says Paul Haller, "you give the next person you meet a beautiful gift."

BE AUTHENTIC

On the one hand, grief is a totally ordinary event. The instant two people meet contains the certainty of their separation. This is the law of loss that rules every human encounter, because transition is constant. "If you mourn a lot when something dies, then you have to mourn every day, many times a day, because something is dying every second, every moment," says Thich Nhat Hanh.[3]

On the other hand, each person has a unique way of responding to separation. Some weep openly; others don't shed a tear. The appropriate response is the one that is genuine and deeply felt.

Grief demands an authentic response. Like dying, there is no correct way to grieve; there is only *our* way. We miss the father we had only just come to know, the son or daughter taken far too soon, the warmhearted mother now gone forever, the partner loved more than life itself. We mourn and we cry out: why me?

Grief touches the most intimate part of the heart. Others can know what we're feeling only if we choose to tell them—*and* they choose to listen. In grief we desperately need a listening ear. Instead we may get a cold shoulder. When the heart is burdened with grief, society tends to offer little support.

THE STOIC RESPONSE

Change, separation, and loss characterize the human experience, but grief—the emotional consequence of being human—is devalued. Other emotions get exaggerated attention in our society. Movie screens are filled with lust, rage, fear, hate, and greed, but genuine sorrow and sadness are mostly out of the picture. This skewed view hardly reflects social reality. Criminal and domestic violence claim so many victims in today's America that grief counselors are regular features in urban elementary schools.

Grief remains a social blind spot because it is the evidence of death, and our social norms are structured to exclude death from awareness. Like the emperor's new clothes, death is socially invisible.

Although death can be concealed, it can't be denied. When death touches us, we're supposed to clench our teeth and stoically wait for the pain to subside. People may say things like "Don't dwell on it. Don't be morbid. It's time to move on. Be active; get on with the job. The children shouldn't see you like this. She's gone; don't talk about her so much. Isn't it wonderful he no longer suffers?"

Even worse is being seen as "just" a daughter-in-law or "just" a neighbor or "just" a partner in a same-sex relationship or just someone else whose grief lacks social standing.

Meanwhile, as the world goes about its business, we may suffer disturbing physical symptoms. There may be butterflies in the stomach, nausea, and shortness of breath. Food can turn tasteless and sleep become fitful and full of strange dreams. Thoughts of disbelief and even self-destruction arise as we cycle through tumultuous feelings. Are we going crazy?

Not really. We're just struggling with a raging sense of loss.

Mourning rituals provide an essential outlet for grief. Memorial services, funerals, wakes, mourning dress, and other cultural expressions evolved to focus and purge the grief reaction in the critical postdeath period of crisis. These ceremonies play a healthy part in the grief process by allowing survivors to affirm their love for the deceased while also affirming their continuing commitment to life.

FINDING MERCY

To grieve is normal because every day, every moment, something is dying, including us. The self longs to survive; the reality of permanent change and loss is troubling. Perceiving our lives as slipping away, we try to grasp and hold on even though separation is certain. And we grieve; we grieve because we're human.

When the pain of loss becomes too much to bear, we can always ask for mercy.

I was reminded of mercy's power at a memorial service for Leroy Hithe. Leroy was an intelligent and socially gifted man who managed to survive many years in prison with his essential innocence intact. He made many hospice friends before he died a quiet, peaceful death.

"Mercy, mercy," murmured the preacher at Leroy's memorial service. "Mercy, mercy," chorused the large crowd of mourners. The plea seemed to be answered in the asking. The cold barn of the chapel filled with a warm sense of the full ripeness of God.

And that's how mercy works. In the very act of asking, mercy is delivered. It takes a certain amount of humility, and even desperation, but when you're willing to get down and admit you can't make anything happen on your own, mercy's bountiful harvest falls into your hands.

Be merciful and embrace your grief. Remember, grief can be a life-threatening condition. If you deny it, you may not live at all. Enter grief fully and you can pass through the crisis and move on to the next phase of your life. Have mercy on yourself and grieve.

DON'T ATTEMPT IT ALONE

Every grieving process is unique. No one can grieve for you, but others can help get the job done. Help is close at hand through hospice. Society may be afraid of grief, but hospice is not. The hospice team that was there for your loved one is now there for you and your loved one's close friends and relatives.

Follow-up is built in. Through phone calls, letters, and personal contact, hospice staff will support mourners for at least one year after the death. Services provided typically include a trained volunteer or counselor making regular visits and the opportunity to participate in peer support groups. Hospice staff will make referrals if chronic depression or other serious grief-induced problems make professional care necessary.

The other ready resource for caregivers is the group of friends and family that came together around the patient. After the last rites are over, there is a tendency for this community to drift apart. Members of the caregiving community should take care of each other. Get in touch and stay in touch for at least six months. Two years or more may have to pass to make a complete adjustment to the loss of a family member or close friend, but the first six months are usually the hardest.

Members of the group should give to each other the empathetic listening they gave to the dying person. It takes solitude to heal the wound of grief at the deepest level, but talking with others is also important. And listening to others describe how their grief is affecting them helps us recognize these events in ourselves.

Because grief isn't one particular emotion or kind of behavior, it can take hold without our really noticing. Use the collective skills of the group to gently engage those who are tightly withdrawn, but avoid being obtrusive. People in pain need privacy. Those troubled by deep questions of meaning may want to talk with a spiritual guide, such as a rabbi, minister, or priest.

Set up a telephone buddy system for people to check in with each other, and be sure to include those living outside the area. Grief tends to dull awareness of the needs of the body. Make sure everyone is getting enough exercise, rest, and good food. Share the work of survival tasks, such as preparing meals, cleaning the house, and caring for children.

Schedule at least one group meeting within the six-month period to share memories, laughter, and tears and move toward closure. This might be the time to distribute the loved one's personal belongings in a final ritual of parting. Send photos and a report of the meeting to those who can't attend.

When you meet together, sit in a circle on chairs or on the floor for fifteen or twenty minutes of silence. Group meditation can be a very powerful support for people in mourning. Reading poetry or listening to music are other ways to draw hearts together.

CHILDREN IN GRIEF

In talking with children about death, we naturally want to shield them from the full impact, but it's very important to explain the details clearly so they won't make up troubling stories that haunt them the rest of their lives.

Children go through a special grieving process. They are especially vulnerable to assuming guilt. ("Mom died because I didn't love her enough.") Tell them the facts. If, in the shock of the moment, they don't fully absorb the explanation, patiently repeat it as they start to open up. Be prepared to do this many times.

When you talk with children about death, describe the deceased person as dead, not lost or passed away, and certainly not as asleep. Any language that obscures the actual reality can have damaging repercussions in a child's later life. Acknowledge that adults don't know everything about death. Share feelings of sadness and anger in a way that reassures the children that they are not alone.

Don't assume that a calm, quiet child isn't full of sorrow. Children are not as verbal as adults. Instead of talking about their grief, they may bottle it up or act it out in ways that are seen as disruptive. Inform friends, teachers, and others in the bereaved child's life about what she is going through.

Like everyone, children need to be heard and understood. A space for comfort and communication can be created by reading to the grieving child from the children's books on death and dying listed in Recommended Reading. Older children may want to read these books on their own.

If adult friends and family are too full of grief to extend support to a grieving child, professional help should be sought. Many hospice programs offer support groups where children can meet with others of their own age and express difficult feelings.

A PRACTICAL MATTER

Grief can feel like a wave that knocks us off our feet and carries us out to sea. We fear there's no way back, but it is possible to "get there from here" if we don't panic. Take a breath and make the trip home a practical matter. Getting into activity helps stop the downward spiral that leads to deep depression.

Grieving is an intensely personal experience; we need to find concrete ways of working with it that are right for us. Bereavement counselors design specific programs of treatment with detailed instructions regarding medication, diet, exercise, and appropriate grieving practices. Caregivers can support each other by sharing their own creative ways of expressing grief's emotions.

Here are a few ways of working with grief suggested by Anne Grant, at KAIROS Support for Caregivers, in San Francisco:

+ Engaging in vigorous physical exercise or work activity
+ Drawing, painting, or sculpting
+ Writing or reading poetry
+ Performing or watching music or interpretive dance
+ Keeping a grief journal or writing an ongoing letter to the loved one
+ Writing a specific letter to express anger, putting everything you feel into the letter and then editing it before sending, or not sending it at all
+ Doing relaxation exercises, meditation, prayer, or massage
+ Participating in or creating rituals
+ Shouting or screaming in your car or on an empty beach

STAGES OF GRIEVING

According to Grant and others, those working with grief must struggle through an initial stage of shock and a prolonged period of suffering before they can achieve renewal and fully reenter life.

Shock.

In the first stage, grief is felt as a sharp, numbing blow. Just as the injured body restricts the flow of blood to stanch further loss, the mind recoils in shock against the trauma caused by death. This stage is expressed in a poem by Norman Fischer.[4]

> People disappear like factory clouds
> Slowly at first but now with the speed of a cloak
> I am reminded that life is a dream, does dissolve
> And sit at the window in shock staring at the smoke

Be grateful for your pain; it helps locate the hurt so treatment can be brought to bear. In this first stage of grieving, the task is to pass through shock and recognize deeply, at the most physical level, the painful truth that the loved one is dead.

Our pervasive death denial tends to dull this awareness. Keeping the body at home with the family after death will help make the loss real. (Details of how to do this should be worked out well in advance.) The funeral industry has popularized the notion that bodies should be made attractive, but it's better for mourners to see the convincing evidence that death has occurred. Seeing is knowing. This is especially true for children, who are easily influenced by their strong imaginations.

If the body is seriously disfigured, photographs placed by the bed can tell the story of the way things were. Those unable to come and spend time with the body may want to take up the practice of contemplating a photo or a memento of the loved one to bring forth blocked feelings.

During this initial period of grief, mourners tend to be more concerned about the dead person than about themselves. The after-death practices of many religions spring from this concern. There is an intense desire to do whatever can be done for the dead. There is love in this, but there is also an essential ritualized purging of our pain.

Eventually the eye of the hurricane passes and the full force of the gale hits us. As shock fades and pain intensifies, raw cravings for the lost loved one may alternate with angry feelings of wanting to shut out her memory altogether. This wild cycle of feelings carries us into the next stage of grieving.

Suffering.

In the first stage we opened our eyes to the grief in the path. In the second stage we invite grief into our hearts. The body armor softens and allows the pain to penetrate fully. "You can't get around death; you have to go through it," says Ajahn Amaro,[5] and the same is true of grief. We go through grief by letting it go through us.

Remaining open to grief is an epic struggle. Weeping buckets of tears may not seem like warrior's work, but it does take real courage to let pain have its way with us. When the dark night of the soul descends, it may seem like every cell in the body wants to cut and run. But escape isn't possible. Fear, anger, and sorrow will dog our every step until we turn back and accept our situation.

Acceptance isn't the same as approval. We don't have to *like* the grief injected into our lives, but we do have to learn how to live with it. If this seems like an unfair request—if the death of a loved one brings a resentful sense of life's injustice—we need to examine our expectations. We aren't born into life on our terms. Taken on its own terms, life is always fair. In the big picture there is room for everything, even death, even fear, even sobbing with grief.

But the tears don't go on endlessly. The body needs a break, so it tunes out the pain. After these periods of rest, we're thrust right back into it again. Grieving is a fluctuating cycle.

Step back and give your grief room to dissipate. Pain causes contraction, and contraction generates explosive pressure. The loss of a loved one is felt as a loss of air and space. The chest tightens, the lungs shrink, and the breath becomes short. Use meditation to relax your breath and release your grief into A Bigger Container.

Stepping back is not detaching but rather expanding awareness to include everything. Grief shrinks our perspective. Wherever we go the walls close in. Even at the edge of the ocean, we find ourselves staring down at the sand. Allow yourself a vision of life large enough to include more than your pain.

The Tibetans have a practice of looking into the sky to cultivate a larger frame of reference. Tibet is on top of the world, and the view must be marvelous, but we don't have to go there; the sky is available everywhere. All you have to do is lift your head and "merely observe." Find a backyard, a park, or a rooftop where you won't be bothered. Settle down in a comfortable lawn chair with your head and neck supported by pillows, and fix your eyes on the great blue yonder. Observing the sky, imagine your grief as a dark stream of smoke that rises and dissolves in thin air. Do this on a regular basis and even your dreams will get bigger!

A loved one's death can shrink our view of life, but nothing can reduce life itself. We grieve to heal and become fully alive. Forgiveness is a healing balm. Let go of anger; let go of guilty thoughts about surviving your loved one; let go of worries about mistakes you wish you hadn't made. Cherish the sense of completeness that comes from knowing you did your best to help your loved one live more fully.

We grieve to forgive but not to forget. We can never really forget; our memories are part of who we are. The task is to find a nurturing relationship with the memory of loss by bringing compassionate awareness to the injury. Grief is healed when the memory of loss is free from pain.

Renewal.

Grief remains unresolved until we accept the loss, but when we do, it transforms us. As we grope our way out of the disorienting loss of a loved one, we discover a liberating new set of priorities. Having learned to accommodate and heal the pain of loss, we reenter life with a keen new awareness.

The kaleidoscope turns. The world that death broke apart comes back together in a different way, and we can see that the journey of grief was a rite of passage. The wound was also an opening. The pain of losing another was the pain of discovering our own mortality. By identifying fully with our loved ones' death we achieved a larger identity. Now we know with a certainty that we too will pass away because we are a part of everything.

This hard-earned awareness puts everything in perspective. We may still fear death—after all, we're human—but we no longer fear *life*. In learning to surrender our loved ones to death, we learn to surrender to life.

It may be hard to believe that enduring grief and accepting its pain leads to a larger sense of life. But it does. This poem by David Whyte expresses the importance of grieving fully.[6]

Those who will not slip beneath
the still surface on the well of grief

turning downward through its black water
to the place we cannot breathe

will never know the source from which we drink,
the secret water, cold and clear,

nor find in the darkness glimmering
the small round coins
thrown by those who wished for something else.

Home Skill: Creating the Home Altar

In grieving we seek to experience fully all the loss that belongs to us so we can heal and become whole. Through painful intimacy with ourselves we renew the possibility of having intimacy with others. One place where we can safely express to ourselves our feelings of grief is before the home altar. As Reb Anderson says, this is the "home within your home." The following guidelines draw on his instructions for setting up a home altar.[7]

1. Set up the altar in a place that is personal to you, so you can be refreshed by it without disturbing others.

2. Build the altar around a meaningful central image. This does not have to be a human figure. It can be anything that has deep significance for you.

3. To the left of the image put a candle and to the right, a flower. (When you can't get a fresh one, use a silk or straw flower.)

4. Place an incense bowl in front of the image. Any small bowl is fine. Fill it with sand, a fine grain like cracked rice, or ash from the fireplace, so it will hold the stick of incense. As the incense ash builds up, you can use this to hold the incense stick.

5. The candlelight, the flower, and the incense serve as offerings. In addition you can offer teachings which you say yourself. These may be favorite poems, hymns, chants, or selections from a sacred book. The important thing is that the words speak your heart's aspirations.

6. As a way to offer yourself, bow to the altar. This is not bowing down to the image on the altar but rather honoring all that your tender heart longs for. "When bowing," says Anderson, "you go down to the earth; you touch the earth with your feet, your knees, your hands, and your head."

III

Inquiring Mind

We do not exist for the sake of something else.
We exist for the sake of ourselves.

—Shunryu Suzuki-roshi

Thirteen

Living Our Dying

Awakened within a dream,
I fall into my own arms.
. . . What kept you so long?

—Lou Hartman

PEOPLE ARE OFTEN SURPRISED by the joy and enthusiasm I have for taking care of the dying. They think of the work as dreary, but anyone who does it knows how much lightness it imparts. Caregiving provides a rare opportunity to shed pretense and self-protection. We unbuckle our sword and lay down our shield of self-importance. Death just makes the games too obvious.

Dying wakes us up to a richer vision of who we are. Seen from the deathbed, wealth, power, and possessions shrink in comparison with personal relationships, nature, spirit, and the simple beauty of another breath. "If I'd only known," a dying man told me in his last hours.

As caregivers we *do* know. But *what* do we know?

It's not easy to describe. The new sensitivity is subtle. There's a heightened awareness that adds zest to life's little pleasures. When we know how fleeting life is, ordinary events seem much more enjoyable. There's a well-known story about this delightful awareness.

A man crossing a field encounters a tiger. He flees, the tiger after him. Coming to a cliff, the man desperately catches hold of a vine and swings himself down over the edge. Trembling, he looks up. The tiger is standing there, sniffing. Then the man looks down. Alas, another tiger is waiting below with a hungry expression. Only the vine keeps him from certain death.

He notices two mice, one white and one black, poke their heads out of the cliff above him. He sees them go to the vine and little by little start gnawing away at it. The vine grows visibly thinner.

Then the man spots a luscious strawberry growing nearby. Grasping the vine with one hand, he plucks the red berry with the other. Oh how delicious![1]

Life goes by in such a jittery blur that it's easy to miss the strawberries on the side of the cliff. Knowing that the end is near should cause us to savor the trip.

Isn't it wonderful to be able to read this sentence with a mind unclouded by dementia or painkilling drugs? Isn't it cause for celebration to be able to use the toilet unaided? When arthritis forced Robert Aitken's wife to use a cane, she would exclaim, "What a comfort this cane is!"[2]

Such gratitude seems saintly, but it's really a very practical response to the challenge of being human. Gratitude makes human fulfillment possible. "To bless whatever there is, and for no other reason but simply because it is—that is our raison d'être; that is what we are made for as human beings," writes David Steindl-Rast, a Benedictine monk.[3]

How do we evoke such a spirit? By not turning away from life.

As caregivers we accept dying into our lives. This expands our vision of who we are. We no longer exclude the elderly, the disabled, and the sick as "not me." The words *cancer* and *AIDS* don't cause us to recoil. Suffering is a familiar presence, not a threat.

FROM PAIN TO HAPPINESS

For me the most amazing discovery of caregiving is that we achieve authenticity by not rejecting pain and suffering. Many of us know or have heard about people who have been able to use pain and trauma—the death of a child or a life-threatening disease or a disabling injury—to transform their lives. I had the good fortune to meet one of these inspiring people when I edited the publications of the organization founded by Ed Roberts, the father of the disability rights movement.

When Ed was fourteen, polio left him paralyzed below the neck and dependent on an iron lung for survival. Written off as a "helpless cripple," he worked his way through the painful stages of accepting his violently altered circumstances. In time he emerged to become the head of California's huge vocational rehabilitation department. And then he grew to embody the human aspiration for freedom in the way of Gandhi and Martin Luther King. By the time of his death in 1995, Ed had changed the lives of millions around the world through his organizing, his personal example, and his ceaseless globe-trotting on behalf of people with disabilities.

Energized by humor, commitment, and love, Ed Roberts made it all look easy. It wasn't. A good friend said at Ed's funeral that he "went through the struggles and somehow came out the other side, transcending all the bitterness and self-destructiveness."

I haven't made a study of Ed's early life, but everything about him says he gave up trying to deny his polio and bargain for a better deal. He simply let the truth of his life be what it was. He could accept his disability because he knew it wasn't him. What others thought about him was beside the point. He knew his life was larger than anybody's idea of it, and that's why he loved life so much.

Ed Roberts is remembered as a bold, sometimes confrontational, leader who never backed down. And he was. (One of his more startling political slogans was "piss on pity.") Yet Ed was a man who achieved his rare and precious strength through internal surrender.

We think that guarding ourselves is the best self-protection, but just the opposite is true. In resisting pain, we resist our lives. This dooms us to endless frustration. The more we try to defend, the more vulnerable we become. There is only one way to transcend pain, and it's damned difficult: we must stop resisting it.

Cultivating a deep connection with a dying person puts us in touch with our pain, and it prods us to wake up. "It isn't pain that awakens us," writes the death and dying teacher Stephen Levine. "Pain is pain and it's a drag! Pain gets our attention. And attention awakens us."[4]

Finally we see compassion as our inner nature, and we make our home there. Having connected deeply with one person, we seek connection with others for the satisfaction it gives us. Caring becomes a reflex. We just naturally want to express our innate generosity because doing so makes us happy. From the sharing of pain emerges the great happiness of living a compassionate life.

REENTRY

Returning to the workaday world after a loved one has died can be a jarring experience.

Now and then in my work as a hospice volunteer I'm asked to go out and buy something for our Friday afternoon happy hour. These trips are unnerving. It's not pleasant to trade a calm, caring atmosphere for the hard-edged affluence of the local supermarket, jammed as it is with shoppers chasing after brightly packaged commodities.

Getting in harmony with our compassion tends to put us out of sync with the prevailing values of consume and compete. This shouldn't, though, make us indifferent toward those whose suffering isn't as obvious as the suffering of the sick and the dying. The Buddha perceived that *all* life is suffering.

Strangely enough, this is good news. It means my suffering is not unique. We're all in this together, and we can all get out of it, too. But first we have to acknowledge the ways we make ourselves suffer.

We suffer because we want. We want a new car or a better job or a more exciting relationship or a stronger body, but with every want we manage to satisfy, another rises up. It's like ducks in a shooting gallery. The wheels go round and round, but dissatisfaction remains constant.

This is suffering. Letting go of suffering sounds easy until we realize that it means letting go of wanting, and we can't do that.

Actually it's not wanting that causes our worst suffering but rather striving to grasp life and work our will on it. Caregiving helps us loosen our grip and let life be. Serving others we serve ourselves. Turning toward the unloved, the painful, and saying yes, this too belongs, this is part of nature and part of me, we become totally who we are.

On their deathbeds famous teachers have made dramatic last gestures or statements expressing their essential teaching. One threw his pillow through a window just before he died; another sat bolt upright and declared, "Don't be misled! Look directly!" Another said simply, "I don't want to die." I find this range of responses tremendously inspiring. It means it's OK to be yourself all the way to the end.

Being yourself doesn't mean being complacent. "You are perfect as you are," Suzuki-roshi was fond of saying. "And you could use a little improvement." All of us have work to do, and the work of living and the work of dying are not different.

When death knocks, some respond by kicking the door. Others welcome death as the way to complete their lives. We, the living, face similar options. Fearing insecurity and discomfort, we can try to flee, or we can turn and squarely face what our lives are. In this way we move toward achieving our full potential despite any pain that stands in the way.

When the will to live truthfully becomes stronger than our fear of pain, pain nurtures our life and we grow.

THE JOY OF IMPERMANENCE

In the Western view, death is the negation of life, but in fact life and death are inseparable. In living there is dying, and in dying there is living. Like burning candles, we are consumed in the process of being who we are. This is why caregiving is all about helping people live fully to the end. After they're gone we're left with a greater awareness of our transience.

Once while I was participating in a memorial service, I had the startling experience of perceiving everyone around me as destined to die. One by one I saw each face replaced by another. This vision disturbed me, but when I raised it with my wise friend Norman Fischer, he wasn't upset in the slightest. "We don't die," Norman said with a laugh. "We just get recycled."

There is wry humor in our impermanence, but there is also a solemn warning. Don't waste time, admonishes a Zen teaching. Zen traces its origins to a moment when the Buddha wordlessly held up a flower and one of his disciples got the point. These days Dr. Bernie Siegel makes the same point, perhaps unwittingly, when he begins his popular talks on healing by holding up a baby to his audience. The point is this: both the flower and the baby are beautiful. And both are transient. "For every three out of ten born," writes Lao-tzu, "three out of ten die."[5]

Knowing that life is fleeting does not dull our taste for it but instead gives new gusto to the experience. Our heightened sense of approaching death brings with it a joyful surprise at continued life. We see that the challenge is not to change life but to settle into its constantly changing circumstances. Transience rules in every realm. "We live in a burning world, in which we are ourselves burning," wrote the scholar R. H. Blyth.[6]

Existence is a parade of extremely short-lived events. Like the separate frames in a moving picture, each moment of consciousness is distinct. Taken together they form a continuous stream of life and death. When we're alert and awake, we're alive to our lives. When we're lost in thoughts or feelings, we're dead. What we call life is actually a mix of these separate life and death elements.

Modern medicine seeks to honor life by attacking death with money and manpower. Through caregiving we learn to honor life by accepting it as it is. And life can't be life without death.

A GREAT DAY TO DIE

Caregiving lets us see our limits. Birth and death are two bookends, supporting us in life. "Look closely," a teacher advised a dying student. "If there were no birth there would be no death."[7] Aware that death helps define us, we cease struggling to avoid it. Certain that life doesn't go on forever, we receive it as a gift.

The paradox is this: the more deeply we penetrate death, the more existence means to us. Caregiving grounds us on the certainty of our mortality, and that changes everything. Knowing in our bones that we will die, we come home to who we are, and we are filled with a sense of freedom. In the words of the Sioux medicine man Lame Deer, "You know, today would be a great day to die!"[8]

These wonderful insights can get easily clouded. The breakthrough in consciousness that caregiving makes possible requires renewal. Each morning we are born into the day, and each evening we fall asleep and die into the night. In between, it's up to us to stay awake.

Whenever I drift toward forgetting my mortality, I can always wake myself up with this poem written by Sue Ellen Balston, a hospice patient.

> Today is
> > Yesterday's tomorrow—
> Full of lost dreams,
> > No longer hoped for.
> Goodbye tomorrows
> > and yesterdays.
> Quit dreaming,
> > you fool,
> And live now!

Appendix 1
Resources

Your hospice, the local American Cancer Society chapter, the AIDS service organizations in your area, and the American Association of Retired Persons, in Washington, D.C., can direct you to a vast array of hospice-related agencies, services, publications, and audio- and videotapes. This list does not attempt to reproduce information that can be easily obtained through those sources. Rather, it is a limited selection of items which I've found particularly helpful.

INTERNET

http://hospice-cares.com
email: healing@hospice-cares.com

The electronic global village is highly responsive to the needs of dying people and their caregivers. Hospice-related mailing lists, chat rooms, and Web sites

abound. My favorite Web page is Hospice Hands, a wisely chosen set of links lovingly updated every week by Jim Nash, R.N., under the auspices of Hospice of North Central Florida.

PRACTICAL CARE

Primer of Palliative Care, Porter Storey, M.D., 1994, 57 pages, $4.95, including shipping. Available from:

The American Academy of Hospice and Palliative Medicine
P.O. Box 14288
Gainesville, FL 32604-2288
(352) 377-8900

The American Academy of Hospice and Palliative Medicine publishes this clearly written introductory guide for medical personnel new to hospice. I can't recommend it too highly for the home caregiver.

CAREGIVING FROM THE HEART

AIDS Caregiving: Lessons for the Second Decade, Charles Garfield and Cindy Spring (two audiocassettes), $5.00, shipping included. Order from:

Impact AIDS
440 Cerrillos Road
Suite F
Santa Fe, NM 87501

Drawn from his extensive work with AIDS caregivers, Dr. Garfield gives heartfelt and well-reasoned advice applicable to anyone tending to the needs of a terminally ill person. This professionally produced, high-quality tape is a pleasure to listen to and comes at a bargain price.

MASSAGE

Service Through Touch, founded by Irene Smith.
A pioneer in massage therapy, Irene Smith has been teaching hands how to heal for over a decade. To obtain a catalog of her audio- and videotapes, contact:

Innerlight Productions
P.O. Box 21478
Oakland, CA 94620
(800) 537-6767

NUTRITION

Food, The Essence of Life: Creative Cooking for the Pureed Diet, The Dietary Department of The Connecticut Hospice, $30 plus shipping and handling from:

Publications Department
The Connecticut Hospice, Inc.
61 Burban Drive
Branford, CT 06405
800-8-HOSPICE

Drawing on the experience of the first American hospice, the book offers institutional and home cooks more than 100 recipes plus other food preparation ideas for the person having trouble eating.

The Non-Chew Cookbook,
J. Randy Wilson, $23.95. Order through your bookstore, or write:
Wilson Publishing
P.O. Box 2190
Glenwood Springs, CO 81602

Eating without chewing—is this possible? Yes, indeed. I can't give you a tasty sample, but here's a recipe taken from the book.

Onion, Cheese, and Egg Bake

4 onions, finely chopped
6 eggs
1 green pepper, finely chopped

6 tablespoons whole milk
10 oz. cheddar cheese, grated
2 tablespoons Worcestershire sauce

Cook the onion in lightly salted boiling water for 5 minutes. Drain.
Place half in oven-proof dish. Sprinkle with half the chopped pepper, then half the cheese. Repeat layers. Beat remaining ingredients together, with salt and pepper to taste. Pour into dish and bake at 350 degrees for 30 minutes. Makes 6 servings.

ADVANCE DIRECTIVES

Shape Your Health Care Future with Health Care Advance Directives, stock no. D15803, $2.00, including shipping. Order from:

AARP-AD
P.O. Box 51040
Washington, DC 20091

The American Medical Association, American Bar Association, and American Association of Retired Persons (AARP)) collaborated to develop this generic advance directive guide with a single form combining the living will and the health care power of attorney. AARP also publishes

several related booklets on the personal, legal, and ethical aspects of communicating preferences about future medical treatment.

PAIN CONTROL

Questions and Answers About Pain Control: A Guide for People with Cancer and Their Families, National Cancer Institute and the American Cancer Society, free.
To obtain a free copy of this or any other American Cancer Society pamphlet, call (800) 227-2345.

VIDEO RESPITE

Video Respite, a series of interactive videotapes for people with dementia, 30 to 60 minutes in length, $30–$60. For a catalog:

Innovative Caregiver Resources
P.O. Box 17332
Salt Lake City, UT 84117
(801) 272-9446

Described as *"Barney* for adults," these videos ask questions and then pause for the patient's responses. The tapes, which are aimed at diverse ethnic audiences, provide respite for the caregiver by keeping the patient stimulated and entertained.

HOSPICE HELPLINE

1-800-658-8898

When you call this number at the National Hospice Organization, in Arlington, Virginia, a real person—not a machine—answers. Now, that's quality care!

NEW APPROACHES TO DEATH AND DYING

Zen Hospice Project
273 Page Street
San Francisco, CA 94102
(415) 863-2910

Living/Dying Project
P.O. Box 357
Fairfax, CA 94978
(415) 456-3915

Spiritual Care for Living and Dying
c/o Rigpa
P.O. Box 607
Santa Cruz, CA 95061
(408) 454-9103

Located within two hours of each other, these three centers have pioneered important new practical and spiritual approaches to death and dying. Each has a distinct orientation. Zen Hospice Project arose out of the San Francisco Zen Center, the Living/Dying Project grew out of the work of Stephen Levine and Ram Dass, and Spiritual Care for Living and Dying is founded on the Tibetan Buddhist teachings of Sogyal Rinpoche.

The Project on Being with Dying
c/o Upaya
1404 Cerro Bordo
Santa Fe, NM 87501
(505) 986-8518

This program is located at a Buddhist retreat center and emphasizes contemplative approaches to working with death in an open and effective manner. It offers training and support to health care professionals, people with severe illness, and caregivers.

꙰

Appendix 2

Song of Lovingkindness*

This is what should be accomplished by the one who is wise, who seeks the good and has obtained peace:

Let one be strenuous, upright and sincere, without pride, easily contented and joyous.
Let one not be submerged by the things of the world.
Let one not take upon one's self the burden of riches.
Let one's senses be controlled.
Let one be wise but not puffed up, and let one not desire great possessions, even for one's family.
Let one do nothing that is mean or that the wise would reprove.

May all beings be happy.
May they be joyous and live in safety.

All living beings, whether weak or strong, in high or middle or low realms of existence, small or great, visible or invisible, near or far, born or to be born, may all beings be happy.

Let no one deceive another, nor despise any being in any state; let none by anger or hatred wish harm to another.

Even as a mother at the risk of her life watches over and protects her only child, so with a boundless mind should one cherish all living things, suffusing love over the entire world, above, below, and all

* Lovingkindness is the translation of *metta,* a word in the ancient Indian dialect of Pali that has two roots: "gentle" and "friend." These verses are also known as the Metta Sutta.

around, without limit; so let one cultivate an infinite good will toward the whole world.

Standing or walking, sitting or lying down, during all one's waking hours, let one practice the way with gratitude

Not holding to fixed views, endowed with insight, freed from sense appetites, one who achieves the way will be freed from the duality of birth and death.

— Translated by San Francisco Zen Center

Appendix 3

Nirvana, the Waterfall

by Shunryu Suzuki-roshi

If you go to Japan and visit Eiheiji monastery, just before you enter you will see a small bridge called Hanshaku-kyo, which means "Half-Dipper Bridge." Whenever Dogen-zenji [Zen Master Dogen] dipped water from the river, he used only half a dipperful, returning the rest to the river again, without throwing it away. That is why we call the bridge Hanshaku-kyo, "Half-Dipper Bridge." At Eiheiji when we wash our face, we fill the basin to just seventy percent of its capacity. And after we wash, we empty the water towards, rather than away from, our body. This expresses respect for the water. This kind of practice is not based on any idea of being economical. It may be difficult to understand why Dogen returned half of the water he dipped to the river. This kind of practice is beyond our thinking. When we feel the beauty of the river, when we are one with the water, we intuitively do it in Dogen's way. It is our true nature to do so. But if your true nature is covered by ideas of economy or efficiency, Dogen's way makes no sense.

I went to Yosemite National Park, and I saw some huge waterfalls. The highest one there is 1,340 feet high, and from it the water comes down like a curtain thrown from the top of the mountain. It does not seem to come down swiftly, as you might expect; it seems to come down very slowly because of the distance. And the water does not come down as one stream, but is separated into many tiny streams. From a distance it looks like a curtain. And I thought it must be a very difficult experience for each drop of water to come down from the top of such a high mountain. It takes time, you know, a long time, for the water finally to reach the bottom of the waterfall. And it seems to me that our human life may be like this. We have many difficult experiences in our life. But at the same time, I thought, the water was not originally separated, but was one whole river. Only when it is separated does it have some difficulty in falling. It is as if the water does not have any feeling when it is one whole river. Only when separated into many drops can it begin to have or to express some feeling. When we see one whole river we do not feel the living activity of the water, but when we dip a part of the water into a dipper, we experience some feeling of the water, and we also feel the value of the person who uses the water. Feeling ourselves and the water in this way, we cannot use it in just a material way. It is a living thing.

Before we were born we had no feeling; we were one with the universe. This is called "mind-only," or "essence of mind," or "big mind." After we are separated by birth from this oneness, as the water falling from the waterfall is separated by the wind and rocks, then we have feeling. You have difficulty because you have feeling. You attach to the feeling you have without knowing just how this kind of feeling is created. When you do not realize that you are one with the river, or one with the universe, you have fear. Whether it is separated into drops or not, water is water. Our life and death are the same thing. When we realize this fact we have no fear of death anymore, and we have no actual difficulty in our life.

When the water returns to its original oneness with the river, it no longer has any individual feeling to it; it resumes its own nature, and finds composure. How very glad the water must be to come back to the original river! If this is so, what feeling will we have when we die? I think we are like the water in the dipper. We will have composure then, perfect composure. It may be too perfect for us, just now, because we are so much attached to our own feeling, to our individual existence. For us, just now, we have some fear of death, but after we resume our true original nature, there is Nirvana. That is why we say, "To attain Nirvana is to pass away." "To pass away" is not a very adequate expression. Perhaps "to pass on," or "to go on," or "to join" would be better. Will you try to find some better expression for death? When you find it, you will have quite a new interpretation of your life. It will be like my experience when I saw the water in the big waterfall. Imagine! It was 1,340 feet high!

We say, "Everything comes out of emptiness." One whole river or one whole mind is emptiness. When we reach this understanding we find the true meaning of our life. When we reach this understanding we can see the beauty of human life. Before we realize this fact, everything that we see is just delusion. Sometimes we overestimate the beauty; sometimes we underestimate or ignore the beauty because our small mind is not in accord with reality.

To talk about it in this way is quite easy, but to have the actual feeling is not so easy. But by your practice of zazen you can cultivate this feeling. When you can sit with your whole body and mind, and with the oneness of your mind and body under the control of the universal mind, you can easily attain this kind of right understanding. Your everyday life will be renewed without being attached to an old erroneous interpretation of life. When you realize this fact, you will discover how meaningless your old interpretation was, and how much useless effort you had been making. You will find the true meaning of life, and even though you have difficulty falling upright from the top of the waterfall to the bottom of the mountain, you will enjoy your life.

SHUNRYU SUZUKI was already a "roshi," or Zen master, when he gave up his position as head of a major temple in Japan to come to America in 1959 and become a priest for a small Japanese congregation in San Francisco. He liked the openness of Americans, and as the city became swept up in the sixties, young people attracted to Eastern religions sought him out. With their help he left Japantown and founded the first American Buddhist community, consisting of several temples and a monastery. He died of cancer in 1971 at age sixty-six. "Nirvana, the Waterfall," is taken from the series of lectures published as *Zen Mind, Beginner's Mind.*

Recommended Reading

Aitken, Robert. *The Gateless Barrier.* San Francisco: North Point Press, 1990.

———. *Taking the Path of Zen.* San Francisco: North Point Press, 1982.

Barasch, Marc Ian. *The Healing Path: A Soul Approach to Illness.* New York: Putnam, 1993.

Beck, Charlotte Joko. *Everyday Zen: Love and Work.* New York: Harper-Collins, 1989.

———. *Nothing Special: Living Zen.* New York: HarperCollins, 1993.

Boerstler, Richard W. "Meditation and the Dying Process," *Journal of Humanistic Psychology* 26, no. 2 (Spring 1986): 104–24.

Brodkey, Harold. *This Wild Darkness: The Story of My Death.* New York: Holt, 1996.

Buckman, Robert. *I Don't Know What to Do: How to Help and Support Someone Who Is Dying.* New York: Little, Brown, 1989.

Callahan, Daniel. *The Troubled Dream of Life: Living with Mortality.* New York: Simon and Schuster, 1993.

Callanan, Maggie, and Patricia Kelley. *Final Gifts: Understanding the Special Awareness, Needs, and Communications of the Dying.* New York: Poseidon, 1992.

Chagdud Tulku Rinpoche. *Life in Relation to Death.* Junction City, CA: Padma, 1987.

Dossey, Larry. *Meaning and Medicine.* New York: Bantam, 1991.

Duda, Deborah. *Coming Home: A Guide to Dying at Home with Dignity.* New York: Aurora, 1987.

Fitch, Victoria Howard. "Caring for the Elderly." *Shambhala Sun* 1, no. 1. (May June 1992): 4–5, 8.

Recommended Reading
𝒫ꝰ

Frankl, Viktor. *Man's Search for Meaning*. New York: Washington Square, 1985.

Garfield, Charles, with Cindy Spring and Doris Ober. *Sometimes My Heart Goes Numb: Love and Caregiving in a Time of AIDS*. San Francisco: Jossey-Bass, 1995.

Graf von Durckheim, Karlfried. *Hara: The Vital Centre of Man*. London: George Allen and Unwin, 1962.

Hanh, Thich Nhat. *The Miracle of Mindfulness*, rev. ed. Boston: Beacon Press, 1987.

Harrison, Gavin. *In the Lap of the Buddha*. Boston: Shambhala, 1994.

Irion, Paul E. *Hospice and Ministry*. Nashville: Abingdon Press, 1988.

Kabat-Zinn, Jon. *Full Catastrophe Living: Using the Wisdom of Your Body and Mind to Face Stress, Pain, and Illness*. New York: Delacorte, 1990.

———.*Wherever You Go There You Are: Mindfulness Meditation in Everyday Life*. New York: Hyperion, 1994.

Kapleau, Philip, ed. *The Wheel of Life and Death*. New York: Doubleday, 1989.

Kornfield, Jack. *A Path with Heart*. New York: Bantam, 1993.

Kübler-Ross, Elisabeth. *Death: The Final Stage of Growth*. Englewood Cliffs, NJ: Prentice-Hall, 1975.

———. *On Death and Dying*. New York: Macmillan, 1969.

Little, Deborah Whiting. *Home Care for the Dying: A Comprehensive Guide to Physical and Emotional Care*. Garden City, NJ: Dial, 1985.

Middlebrook, Christina. *Seeing the Crab: A Memoir Before Dying*. New York: Basic Books, 1996.

Mitchell, Stephen, ed. *The Enlightened Mind: An Anthology of Sacred Prose*. New York: HarperCollins, 1991.

Mukai, Linda Pratt and Janis Fisher Chan. *Living with Dying*. San Anselmo, CA: Butterfield, 1996.

Nuland, Sherwin B. *How We Die: Reflections on Life's Final Chapter*. New York: Knopf, 1994.

Ryokan. *Ryokan: Zen Monk-Poet of Japan*. Trans. Burton Watson. New York: Columbia University Press, 1977.

Saigyo. *Mirror for the Moon.* Trans. William R. LaFleur. New York: New Directions, 1977.

Salzberg, Sharon. *Lovingkindness: The Revolutionary Art of Happiness.* Boston: Shambhala, 1995.

Sankar, Andrea. *Dying at Home.* Baltimore: Johns Hopkins University Press, 1991.

Smith, Irene. "Bodywork for People with HIV." *Massage and Bodywork Quarterly* (Spring 1994): 37–44.

Snyder, Gary. *Riprap and Cold Mountain Poems.* San Francisco: North Point Press, 1990.

Sogyal Rinpoche. *The Tibetan Book of Living and Dying.* New York: HarperCollins, 1992.

Storey, Porter. *Primer of Palliative Care.* Gainesville, FL: The American Academy of Hospice and Palliative Medicine, 1994.

Suzuki, Shunryu. *Zen Mind, Beginner's Mind.* New York: Weatherhill, 1970.

Tanahashi, Kazuaki, and Tensho David Schneider, eds. *Essential Zen.* New York: HarperCollins, 1994.

Tatelbaum, Judy. *The Courage to Grieve: Creative Living, Recovery, and Growth Through Grief.* New York: Harper and Row, 1980.

Tolstoy, Leo. *The Death of Ivan Illich.* Available in various editions.

CHILDREN'S BOOKS

Krementz, Jill. *How It Feels When a Parent Dies.* New York: Knopf, 1981. Eighteen young people ranging in age from seven to seventeen talk about their grief and fears after one of their parents died.

Gerstein, Mordicai. *The Mountains of Tibet.* New York: Harper and Row, 1987. A picture book explaining Tibetan Buddhist teachings about reincarnation.

Viorst, Judith. *The Tenth Good Thing About Barney.* New York: Simon and Schuster, 1987. When a little girl loses her cat, her father helps her come to terms with her feelings.

Wilhelm, Hans. *I'll Always Love You.* New York: Crown, 1985. A boy's sadness over his dog's death is tempered by remembering to say every night, "I'll always love you."

$\mathscr{L}$

Notes

1. WHY YOU SHOULD HELP YOUR LOVED ONE DIE AT HOME

1. Gallup poll cited in *Hospice: A Photographic Inquiry* (Washington, DC: Corcoran Gallery of Art, 1996), n.p.

2. Alfred F. Connors et al., "A Controlled Trial to Improve Care for Seriously Ill Hospitalized Patients," *Journal of the American Medical Association* 274 (1995): 1591–98.

3. Daniel Callahan, "Our Fear of Dying," *Newsweek* (October 4, 1993): 67.

4. U.S. Congress, House Committee on the Judiciary, Subcommittee on the Constitution, "Assisted Suicide in the United States," 104th Congress, 2nd session, 1996, ser. 78, 19.

5. From "Death, Judgment and the Life Hereafter," in *Religion in America, 1992–1993,* as quoted in "We Occasionally Think of Death," *Shambhala Sun* 3, no. 4 (March 1995): 45.

6. U.S. Congress, "Assisted Suicide," 15.

7. Ibid., 20.

8. Deborah Gesensway, "SUPPORT Study Blasts Physicians," *ACP Observer* 16, no. 2 (February 1996): 13.

9. "A Conversation with Dannion Brinkley," *Monthly Aspectarian: Online Edition* (September 1995): http://www.lightworks.com.

10. Charles Garfield, *Sometimes My Heart Goes Numb: Love and Caregiving in a Time of AIDS* (San Francisco: Jossey-Bass, 1995), 72.

11. Kazuaki Tanahashi, ed., *Moon in a Dewdrop* (San Francisco: North Point, 1985), 91.

2. SPIRITUAL CARE IS NOTHING SPECIAL

1. Robert M. Pirsig, *Zen and the Art of Motorcycle Maintenance* (New York: Morrow, 1974), 13.

2. Linda Pratt Mukai and Janis Fisher Chan, *Living with Dying* (San Anselmo, CA: Butterfield, 1996), 156.

3. MEDITATION TAKES CARE OF US

1. Gary Snyder, "Just One Breath," *Tricycle: The Buddhist Review* 1, no. 1 (Fall 1991), 56.
2. Shunryu Suzuki-roshi, "Purely Involved Helping Others," *Windbell* 30, no. 2 (Summer 1996): 3.
3. Yoel Hoffmann, trans. and comp., *Japanese Death Poems* (Rutland, VT: Charles E. Tuttle, 1986), 328.

5. ACCEPTANCE IS EVERYTHING

1. Shunryu Suzuki, *Zen Mind, Beginner's Mind* (New York: Weatherhill, 1970), 30.
2. Ibid., 35.
3. Frank Ostaseski, "Living with the Dying," *Inquiring Mind* 6, no. 2 (Winter–Spring 1990): 10.
4. Mwalimu Imara, "Dying as the Last Stage of Growth," in Elisabeth Kübler-Ross, *Death: The Final Stage of Growth* (Englewood Cliffs, NJ: Prentice-Hall, 1975), 147.

6. GIVING THE GIFT OF LISTENING

1. Thomas Merton, *No Man Is an Island* (New York: Harcourt Brace Jovanovich, 1955), 188.
2. Bharat J. Lindemood with Jacquelyn J. Schechter, "Into the Light: Working with Dying AIDS Patients from a Contemplative Perspective," *Journal of Contemplative Psychotherapy* 8 (1992): 14.
3. The Japanese have developed an extensive analysis and practice of centering attention in the lower belly, or *hara*. See Karlfried Graf von Durkheim, *Hara: The Vital Centre of Man* (London: George Allen and Unwin, 1962).
4. Philip Kapleau, *The Three Pillars of Zen* (Boston: Beacon Press, 1967), 67.

7. THE TAO OF EATING AND ELIMINATION

1. Porter Storey, *Primer of Palliative Care* (Gainesville, FL: Academy of Hospice Physicians, 1994), 23.

2. Ryokan, *Ryokan: Zen Monk-Poet of Japan,* trans. Burton Watson (New York: Columbia University Press, 1977), 67.

3. Andrea Sankar, *Dying at Home* (Baltimore: Johns Hopkins University Press, 1991), 93.

8. EASING PAIN AND LEARNING ITS LESSONS

1. *Questions and Answers About Pain Control: A Guide for People with Cancer and Their Families* (Bethesda, MD: National Cancer Institute and American Cancer Society, n.d.), 4.

2. U.S. Congress, "Assisted Suicide," 20.

3. Philip Kapleau, *The Wheel of Life and Death* (New York: Doubleday, 1989), 118.

4. Robert V. Brody, "Pain Management in Terminal Disease," *Focus: A Review of AIDS Research* 1, no. 6 (May 1986): 1.

5. Garfield, *Sometimes My Heart Goes Numb,* 225–56.

6. Richard W. Boerstler, "Meditation and the Dying Process," *Journal of Humanistic Psychology* 26, no. 2 (Spring 1986): 104–24.

9. TAKING CARE OF FEELINGS

1. Thich Nhat Hanh, "Transformation and Healing," *Karuna* 7, no. 3 (Winter 1990–91): 13.

2. Charlotte Joko Beck, *Everyday Zen: Love and Work* (New York: Harper-Collins, 1989), 49–52.

3. Thich Nhat Hanh, *Peace Is Every Step* (New York: Bantam, 1991), 59–60.

4. Suzuki, *Zen Mind,* 32.

5. Sharon Salzberg, *Lovingkindness: The Revolutionary Art of Happiness* (Boston: Shambhala, 1995), 20.

6. Thich Nhat Hanh, *Living Buddha, Living Christ* (New York: Putnam, 1995), 118.

7. Walter Truett Anderson, *Open Secrets* (Los Angeles: Tarcher, 1979), 101–2.

10. TOUCH IS THE WAY TO CONNECT

1. Larry Dossey, *Meaning and Medicine* (New York: Bantam, 1991), 192.

2. Irene Smith, "Bodywork for People with HIV," *Massage and Bodywork Quarterly* (Spring 1994): 40.

11. A DEATH IN THE FAMILY

1. Garfield, *Sometimes My Heart Goes Numb,* 277.

12. PASSING THROUGH THE GATEWAY OF GRIEF

1. Dossey, *Meaning and Medicine,* 90.

2. Ajahn Amaro, "No Empty Ideal," in *Seeing the Way* (Great Gaddesden, Eng.: Amaravasti Publications, 1989), 174.

3. Thich Nhat Hanh, "Birth, Death and Interbeing," *Karuna* 8, no. 1 (Spring 1991): 6.

4. Norman Fischer, "Versions of Saigyo," *Shambhala Sun* 3, no. 4 (March 1995): 15.

5. Speaking to Zen Hospice Project volunteers, September 7, 1996.

6. David Whyte, "The Well of Grief," in *Where Many Rivers Meet* (Langley, WA: Many Rivers Press, 1996), 35.

7. Tenshin Reb Anderson, *Warm Smiles from Cold Mountains,* ed. Susan Moon (San Francisco: San Francisco Zen Center, 1995), 34.

13. LIVING OUR DYING

1. Paul Reps and Nyogen Senzaki, *Zen Flesh, Zen Bones* (Boston: Shambhala, 1994): 39–40.

2. Robert Aitken, *The Practice of Perfection* (New York: Random House, 1994), 50.

3. David Steindl-Rast, *Gratefulness, the Heart of Prayer: An Approach to Life in Fullness* (Ramsey, NJ: Paulist Press, 1984), 81.

4. Stephen Levine, "Expanding 'My' Pain into 'The Pain,'" *Inquiring Mind* 6, no. 2 (1990): 4.

5. Philip Kapleau, ed., *The Wheel of Death* (New York: Harper and Row, 1971), 12.

6. *Zen and Zen Classics: Selections from R. H. Blyth,* comp. Frederick Franck (New York: Vintage, 1978), 110.

7. Achan Chaa [Ajahn Chah], "Our Real Home," *Shambhala Sun* 2, no. 3 (January 1994), 30.

8. Boerstler, "Meditation and the Dying Process," 123.

ja

Index